ISBN 978-0-265-90729-0
PIBN 11116765

This book is a reproduction of an important historical work. Forgotten Books uses state-of-the-art technology to digitally reconstruct the work, preserving the original format whilst repairing imperfections present in the aged copy. In rare cases, an imperfection in the original, such as a blemish or missing page, may be replicated in our edition. We do, however, repair the vast majority of imperfections successfully; any imperfections that remain are intentionally left to preserve the state of such historical works.

1 MONTH OF
FREE
READING

at

www.ForgottenBooks.com

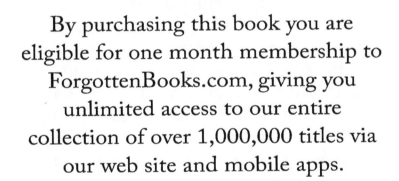

By purchasing this book you are
eligible for one month membership to
ForgottenBooks.com, giving you
unlimited access to our entire
collection of over 1,000,000 titles via
our web site and mobile apps.

To claim your free month visit:

www.forgottenbooks.com/free1116765

CROPS AND MARKETS

Published Monthly by the
United States Department of Agriculture

CERTIFICATE: By direction of the Secretary of Agriculture the matter contained herein is published as statistical information and is required for the proper transaction of the public business. Free distribution is limited to copies "necessary in the transaction of public business required by law." Subscription price $1 a year (foreign rate $1.50), single copy, 10 cents, payable in cash or money order to the Superintendent of Documents, Government Printing Office, Washington, D. C.

WASHINGTON, D. C., JULY 1940   VOL. 17, No. 7

In This Issue

Crops have made a good start and better-than-average yields are indicated by July 1 conditions. Reports on July 1 crop prospects average substantially higher than on the same date last year and nearly as high as 2 years ago; but yields are not expected to be as high as in those years—1938 and 1939—unless the weather during the growing season after July 1 should be equally as favorable. During the first 10 days of July, rainfall has been reported to be deficient in most of the area from Illinois westward, and part of the South reports too much rain.

While crop production has not been increasing in proportion to population, requirements and markets are changing, and stocks of some commodities are so large that supplies of major products are expected to be ample. Present indications are that the production of the various crops this year will give a well-balanced total that will permit utilization of some of the reserves on hand and add little to farm stocks, except hay.

Wheat production—estimated at 729 million bushels—will be a little below average, but with a larger than usual carry-over on farms from last year there will be about the usual supply. There will be about an average supply of potatoes and sweetpotatoes but tobacco production will probably be 30 percent below last year's.

Summary of the Acreage, Yield, and Production of Important Crops, for the United States

Crop	Acreage (in thousands) Harvested Average, 1929–38	1939	For harvest, 1940	1940 percent of 1939	Unit	Yield per acre Average, 1929–38	1939	Indicated July 1, 1940	Production (in thousands) Average, 1929–38	1939	Indicated June 1, 1940	July 1, 1940
	Acres	Acres	Acres			Bushel						
Corn, all.............	98,986	88,803	86,306	97.2	Bushel...	23.2	29.5	28.0	2,299,342	2,610,137	....	2,415,998
Wheat, all...........	55,860	53,696	52,680	98.1	..do......	13.2	14.1	13.8	754,685	754,971	....	728,044
Winter..............	39,453	37,802	34,922	92.4	..do......	14.3	14.9	15.0	571,067	563,431	488,858	523,390
All spring...........	17,416	15,894	17,758	111.7	..do......	10.4	12.1	11.5	183,619	191,540	....	204,654
Durum.............	3,035	3,066	3,330	108.6	..do......	9.1	11.2	10.5	29,619	34,360	....	34,954
Other spring......	14,381	12,828	14,428	112.5	..do......	10.6	12.3	11.8	154,000	157,180	....	169,700
Oats.................	37,005	33,070	34,585	104.6	..do......	27.4	28.3	29.8	1,024,552	997,215	....	1,031,622
Barley...............	10,795	12,600	13,290	105.5	..do......	20.6	21.9	21.6	225,486	276,298	....	287,377
Rye..................	3,250	3,811	3,086	81.0	..do......	11.4	10.3	11.9	38,095	39,349	38,640	36,848
Flaxseed............	1,868	2,284	3,168	138.7	..do......	6.0	8.9	9.1	10,846	20,330	....	28,801
Rice.................	924	1,089	1,095	105.4	..do......	47.9	50.3	49.6	44,254	52,306	....	54,207
Cotton..............	34,929	24,683	25,077	101.6								
Hay, all.............	67,827	69,245	71,551	103.3	Ton......	1.16	1.22	1.32	78,948	84,526	....	94,163
Hay, all tame........	55,808	58,347	60,573	103.8	..do......	1.25	1.30	1.41	69,650	75,726	....	85,301
Hay, wild...........	12,019	10,898	10,978	100.7	..do......	.76	.81	.81	9,298	8,800	....	8,862
Hay, clover and timothy	28,263	20,828	21,788	104.6	..do......	1.12	1.14	1.32	26,030	23,640	....	28,840
Hay, alfalfa..........	12,673	12,494	12,838	102.5	..do......	1.94	2.00	2.20	24,897	27,035	....	30,490
Beans, dry edible....	1,737	1,554	1,751	112.7	Bag.....	759	898	806	13,086	13,962	....	14,111
Soybeans............	4,756	9,023	10,296	114.0								
Cowpeas.............	2,476	2,923	3,059	104.7								
Velvetbeans.........	107	161	167	103.7								
Potatoes............	3,296	3,027	3,067	102.0	Bushel...	111.5	120.3	120.3	366,949	364,016	....	371,263
Sweetpotatoes......	860	862	797	92.5	..do......	84.6	84.3	86.3	72,436	72,679	....	68,800
Tobacco............	1,674	2,014	1,437	71.3	Pound...	816	918	899	1,360,661	1,848,654	....	1,291,685
Sorgo for sirup......	216	180	190	105.6								
Sugarcane for sugar..	249	277	288	104.0	Ton......	17.4	22.4	20.4	4,439	6,197	....	5,874
Sugarcane for sirup..	133	145	123	84.8								
Sugar beets.........	792	917	913	99.6	Ton......	11.3	11.7	11.0	8,937	10,773	....	10,019
Hops...............	29	31	33	105.5	Pound...	1,184	1,270	1,219	34,310	39,380	....	39,868

						Condition July 1						
						Percent	Percent	Percent				
Apples.............						56	64	59				
Peaches, total crop..						58	69	60	52,723	60,822	52,012	52,436
Pears, total crop.....					Bushel...	59	63	65	26,333	31,047	30,653	51,240
Grapes.............					..do......	78	85	78	2,220	2,226	....	2,422
Pasture............					Ton......	73	78	83				
Peanuts............	1,872	2,410	2,493	103.4		72	73	80				
Total (excluding duplication)......	324,309	304,489	305,711	100.7								

[1] Acreage in cultivation July 1.
[2] Excludes sweetclover and lespedeza.
[3] Bag of 100 pounds.
[4] Pounds.
[5] Grown alone for all purposes.
[6] Includes some quantities not harvested.
[7] Condition on July 1 in States having commercial production.
[8] Production includes all grapes for fresh fruit, juice, wine, and raisins.

Planted Acreages of Certain Spring Sown Crops, 1939 and 1940

State	Corn, all		Oats		Barley		Potatoes		All spring wheat		Durum wheat		Other spring wheat		Flaxseed		Beans, dry edible		Sugar beets	
	1939	1940	1939	1940	1939	1940	1939	1940	1939	1940	1939	1940	1939	1940	1939	1940	1939	1940	1939	1940
	1,000 acres	1,000 acres	1,000 acres	1,000 acres	1,000 acres	1,000 acres	1,000 acres	1,000 acres	1,000 acres	1,000 acres	1,000 acres	1,000 acres	1,000 acres	1,000 acres	1,000 acres	1,000 acres	1,000 acres	1,000 acres	1,000 acres	1,000 acres
Maine	14	14	121	116	4	4	170	177												
New Hampshire	15	15	7	7			9.3	9.7	4	4			4	4			11	10		
Vermont	76	75	57	56	5	5	15.0	15.4									3	3		
Massachusetts	38	39	7	7			17.0	18.7												
Rhode Island	10	10	2	2			4.1	4.5												
Connecticut	50	51	7	7			17.5	19.1												
New York	699	713	782	751	146	138	211	215	6	5			6	5			142	154		
New Jersey	189	180	45	43	8	8	55	58												
Pennsylvania	1,368	1,368	906	870	124	150	187	191	10	11			10	11						
Ohio	3,425	3,220	1,109	998	50	55	120	121	5	5			5	5			51	47		
Indiana	4,144	3,987	1,282	1,156	43	60	48	51	9	6			9	6						
Illinois	8,051	7,487	3,430	3,215	172	138	37	38	36	26			36	26						
Michigan	1,574	1,590	1,174	1,233	207	182	250	250	20	18			20	18	8	9	451	539	125	126
Wisconsin	2,233	2,255	2,185	2,251	770	662	197	197	50	46			50	46	11	14	2	2		
Minnesota	4,501	4,321	3,499	4,196	2,136	2,008	243	253	1,452	1,696	72	78	1,380	1,518	1,941	1,554	2	2		
Iowa	8,688	8,816	5,369	5,369	274	408	56	56	40	30			40	30	92	204				
Missouri	4,229	3,933	1,870	1,890	163	170	53	52	3	1			3	1			5			
North Dakota	1,062	1,073	1,616	1,826	1,823	2,055	158	180	8,378	9,105	2,644	2,856	5,734	6,250	504	816				
South Dakota	3,050	3,080	1,908	2,097	1,882	1,995	32	34	2,794	2,989	504	630	2,290	2,359	178	320				
Nebraska	7,425	6,682	1,676	1,826	1,401	1,625	88	87	154	186			154	186	1	2	16	21	80	74
Kansas	3,316	3,150	1,663	1,713	1,200	1,260	30	30	10	35			10	35	101	141	1	2		
Delaware	144	141	3	3			6.0	4.3												
Maryland	506	511	41	35	72	76	25	26												
Virginia	1,405	1,377	80	84	80	84	78	78												
West Virginia	491	486	73	65	10	9	32	32												
North Carolina	2,466	2,441	263	250	11	13	83	81												
South Carolina	1,724	1,789	490	485			28	28												
Georgia	4,346	4,172	426	443			18	19												
Florida	805	821	8	9			3	32												
Kentucky	2,816	2,816	63	65	51	64	46	47												
Tennessee	2,635	2,740	55	80	55	70	41	43												
Alabama	3,550	3,442	132	158			45	48												
Mississippi	3,034	3,009	76	120			20	20												
Arkansas	2,151	2,022	132	145			39	41												
Louisiana	1,588	1,508	52	60			39	37												
Oklahoma	1,972	1,972	1,380	1,449	462	415	45	47	34	34					20	46				
Texas	4,827	5,068	1,488	1,503	263	255	43	47												
Montana	148	155	326	310	230	228	19	18	2,830	3,113			2,830	3,113	166	188	15	18	76	86
Idaho	33	31	169	182	155	183	127	127	306	330			306	330	10	5	111	134	77	77
Wyoming	208	200	126	120	83	85	25	24	135	146			135	146			50	55	63	49
Colorado	1,054	1,000	175	180	625	625	97	89	278	361			278	361			409	389	167	154
New Mexico	219	197	30	30	8		6.0	6.0	26	26			26	26			178	180		
Arizona	28	29	10	10	34	39	2.2	2.4							5	12	10	11		
Utah	19	20	29	28	65	70	12.7	13.1	68	66			68	66					55	51
Nevada	2	4	7	7	15	15	2.0	2.3	17	16			17	16						
Washington	32	29	229	240	96	139	42	42	716	1,002			716	1,002	2					
Oregon	61	55	350	340	177	200	45	46	185	250			185	250					171	180
California	60	63	136	150	1,341	1,274	74	75							114	140	329	358	133	138
Other States																				
United States	91,501	88,116	35,512	35,871	14,546	14,779	3,063.8	3,122.5	17,532	19,374	3,220	3,564	14,312	15,810	2,470	3,458	1,744	1,880	990	982

[1] Revised from December preliminary estimate.

Stocks of Corn, Old Wheat, and Oats on Farms July 1, 1940, With Comparisons

State	Corn for grain						Old wheat						Oats					
	Percent of previous year's crop			Quantity			Percent of previous year's crop			Quantity			Percent of previous year's crop			Quantity		
	Average 1929–38	1939	1940	Average 1929–38	1939	1940	Average 1929–38	1939	1940	Average 1929–38	1939	1940	Average 1929–38	1939	1940	Average 1929–38	1939	1940
				1,000 bu.	1,000 bu.	1,000 bu.				1,000 bu.	1,000 bu.	1,000 bu.				1,000 bu.	1,000 bu.	1,000 bu.
Maine	6	3	8.5	6	4	13	12	20	2.5	12	14		18	21	22	797	814	1,012
New Hampshire	15	23	12	22	38	15							18	20	22	53	53	57
Vermont	11	12	11	40	48	35							14	14	11	267	243	207
Massachusetts	18	9	9	70		25							12	12	20	19	24	46
Rhode Island	20	15	22	13	16	16							14	10	10	9	6	5
Connecticut	19	15	22	100	59	94							9	21	9			
New York	15	16	20	717	1,072	1,246	14	9	13	730	678	830	16	17	19	3,757	4,520	4,903
New Jersey	24	26	27	1,383	1,522	1,488	7	8	8	90	107	94	19	12	14	253	147	176
Pennsylvania	19	20	19	7,626	9,292	8,503	8	6	5	1,550	1,322	1,554	15	15	14	4,183	4,598	3,678
Ohio	17	25	22	28,627	36,850	35,596	9	6	5	3,291	2,785	2,415	12	13	16	5,050	4,809	4,310
Indiana	19	29	25	28,378	47,263	51,217	7	5	4	2,015	1,731	1,104	11	11	10	5,379	5,747	2,522
Illinois	27	52	46	80,246	186,498	186,026	7	3.5	3.5	1,625	1,463	1,366	14	18	12	16,701	16,750	11,225
Michigan	16	25	20	4,985	10,969	9,090	14	18	17	2,202	3,513	2,622	15	17	14	5,885	7,283	7,688
Wisconsin	11	24	19	3,453	10,118	7,610	17	24	21	308	482	284	13	17	14	10,069	12,938	9,942
Minnesota	14	43	49	14,694	52,986	61,895	13	19	22	2,491	7,400	4,864	16	21	18	20,703	27,027	27,297
Iowa	25	59	63	92,958	267,166	303,390	11	16	10	740	1,485	649	16	20	17	31,253	41,804	26,319
Missouri	20	33	26	19,494	34,855	34,374	6	8	3.5	1,847	2,528	1,022	13	18	11	4,539	8,372	4,501
North Dakota	7	15	13	154		432	9	17	21	6,278	12,985	17,653	22	14	30	6,411	10,015	10,589
South Dakota	19	41	46	6,848	12,348	18,225	26	23	26	3,171	6,527	5,050	27	24	22	9,016	11,361	9,664
Nebraska	31	53	59	34,780	53,750	44,041	12	11	15	4,584	6,129	6,648	17	22	17	8,596	13,117	3,498
Kansas	23	30	21	13,927	11,664	6,080	7	7.5	10	9,749	11,414	11,166	12	14	5.5	4,009	4,994	1,165
Delaware	21	17	20	779	685	813	3	2		49	33	13	7	3	2	4	3	2
Maryland	22	22	30	3,182	3,858	3,449	3	6	2.5	285	283	184	11	9	11	161	118	124
Virginia	18	15	17	5,537	5,172	5,808	6	6	4	544	512	451	9	12	8	225	237	104
West Virginia	15	15	15	1,817	1,773	1,962	11	12	10	227	281	210	13	12	14	281	217	204
North Carolina	18	21	23	7,470	9,420	10,697	6	9.1	7.5	277	495	382	7	12	11	281	668	625

Stocks of Corn, Old Wheat, and Oats on Farms July 1, 1940, With Comparisons—Continued

State	Corn for grain						Old wheat						Oats					
	Percent of previous year's crop			Quantity			Percent of previous year's crop			Quantity			Percent of previous year's crop			Quantity		
	Average 1929–38	1939	1940	Average 1929–38	1939	1940	Average 1929–38	1939	1940	Average 1929–38	1939	1940	Average 1929–38	1939	1940	Average 1929–38	1939	1940
				1,000 bu.	1,000 bu.	1,000 bu.				1,000 bu.	1,000 bu.	1,000 bu.				1,000 bu.	1,000 bu.	1,000 bu.
South Carolina	18	23	17	3,790	6,046	4,247	4	2.5	2	40	44	48	5	6.5	5.5	414	692	633
Georgia	15	21	13	5,921	10,964	4,696	5	9	6	54	153	106	6	10	7	402	958	626
Florida	9	15	6	554	1,211	346							3	0	0	4	0	0
Kentucky	17	20	16	11,052	14,607	11,036	3	3.5	1.5	146	304	61	7	14	8.5	187	191	81
Tennessee	17	17	15	10,129	11,392	7,725	3	3.4	2	197	184	82	7	8	5.5	109	136	79
Alabama	15	20	13	9,780	9,780	4,329	4	5	9.5	2	3	7	6	2.5	6	86	190	71
Mississippi	13	15	10	4,909	7,296	3,442							5	1	6	47	18	137
Arkansas	12	14	11	3,885	4,869	3,413	3	3	1.5	22	18	6	5	6	7	168	154	203
Louisiana	7	9	9	1,583	2,357	2,033							4	8	4.5	36	108	75
Oklahoma	9	11	5.5	3,456	3,722	1,685	6	6.5	3.5	2,713	6,009	2,115	9	11	4.5	2,559	3,019	950
Texas	10	10	9	7,890	7,400	6,108	2	2	5	842	701	1,382	12	10	9	4,274	3,692	2,588
Montana	9	22	14	36	242	122	10	17	29	3,527	11,819	16,416	21	26	28	1,398	2,387	2,941
Idaho	16	30	18	132	262	158	8	14	10	1,946	4,526	2,262	12	12	22	575	590	1,371
Wyoming	11	17	4	115	255	35	12	17	16	320	768	450	15	22	19	437	677	433
Colorado	11	21	8	1,654	2,038	508	8	13	16	918	2,479	1,955	16	20	16	738	1,011	673
New Mexico	12	7	13	337	151	280	3	5	2	191	136	59	11	5	10	64	33	64
Arizona	3	5	2	26	20	4	2	1	1	14	11	8	4	0	5	13	0	12
Utah	4	5	5	7	10	8	8	16	7	425	1,074	270	10	10	8	146	109	78
Nevada	2	2	2		1	1	4	10	10	16	52	51	9	10	10	7	28	24
Washington	6	15	5	28	63	21	3	2	2	1,212	1,092	876	10	6	14	820	403	1,571
Oregon	8	15	13	61	126	121	4	3	2	738	705	841	12	7.5	15	1,069	504	1,876
California	1	1	1	17	14	14	1	1	.5	80	127	53	4	1	2	127	34	79
United States	20.1	36.9	36.5	411,942	849,765	662,474	7.4	9.7	11.3	55,165	90,372	85,521	14.5	17.6	15.3	154,595	187,713	143,741

Indicated Yield and Production of Crops July 1, 1940, With Comparisons

State	Corn, all									Oats								
	Acreage			Yield per acre			Production			Acreage			Yield per acre			Production		
	Harvested		For harvest 1940							Harvested		For harvest 1940						
	Average 1929–38	1939		Average 1929–38	1939	Indicated July 1, 1940	Average 1929–38	1939	Indicated July 1, 1940	Average 1929–38	1939		Average 1929–38	1939	Indicated July 1, 1940	Average 1929–38	1939	Indicated July 1, 1940
	1,000 acres	1,000 acres	1,000 acres	Bu.	Bu.	Bu.	1,000 bu.	1,000 bu.	1,000 bu.	1,000 acres	1,000 acres	1,000 acres	Bu.	Bu.	Bu.	1,000 bu.	1,000 bu.	1,000 bu.
Maine	13	14	14	38.7	39.0	38.0	481	546	515	117	121	116	36.7	38.0	36.0	4,316	4,598	4,176
New Hampshire	15	15	15	41.2	41.0	41.0	613	615	615	8	7	7	37.4	37.0	37.0	283	259	259
Vermont	72	76	75	39.8	40.0	38.0	2,873	3,040	2,850	59	57	56	31.1	33.0	31.0	1,849	1,881	1,736
Massachusetts	39	38	39	41.0	40.0	40.0	1,595	1,520	1,560	5	7	7	32.7	33.0	32.0	171	231	224
Rhode Island	9	10	10	39.7	41.0	39.0	354	410	390	2	2	2	31.8	31.0	32.0	64	62	64
Connecticut	52	50	51	38.8	39.0	37.0	1,998	1,950	1,887	7	7	7	29.2	25.0	29.0	193	175	203
New York	641	699	713	34.0	35.0	33.0	21,824	24,465	23,529	828	782	751	27.8	33.0	29.0	23,076	25,806	21,779
New Jersey	190	189	189	38.4	38.0	36.0	7,291	7,182	6,804	46	43	43	29.4	28.0	29.0	1,349	1,260	1,247
Pennsylvania	1,317	1,368	1,368	39.6	42.5	41.0	52,402	58,140	56,088	928	906	870	28.2	29.0	32.0	26,187	26,274	27,840
Ohio	3,608	3,423	3,220	37.2	50.0	41.0	134,812	171,250	132,020	1,449	1,020	968	30.4	32.5	35.0	44,220	33,150	33,880
Indiana	4,446	4,144	3,937	34.1	51.5	42.0	152,216	213,416	165,354	1,946	1,000	1,110	26.3	25.0	34.0	43,698	25,225	37,740
Illinois	8,500	8,051	7,487	34.6	52.0	45.0	311,656	418,652	336,915	3,856	3,118	3,119	30.6	30.0	35.0	119,452	95,540	109,165
Michigan	1,498	1,574	1,590	29.7	37.0	32.0	44,978	58,238	50,880	1,321	1,139	1,207	28.9	37.5	34.5	38,305	42,712	41,642
Wisconsin	2,270	2,233	2,255	32.1	38.5	36.0	72,844	85,970	81,180	2,271	2,185	2,251	30.8	32.5	34.0	76,147	71,012	76,534
Minnesota	4,679	4,501	4,321	29.6	46.5	36.4	138,187	204,796	157,716	4,268	3,939	4,136	30.8	38.5	38.0	132,787	151,652	144,760
Iowa	10,890	9,088	8,816	36.0	52.0	48.0	394,166	503,776	428,168	5,927	5,076	5,262	31.9	30.5	34.0	191,235	154,818	178,908
Missouri	5,346	4,229	3,933	19.9	29.0	28.0	107,663	122,641	110,124	1,651	1,860	1,860	21.2	22.0	22.0	35,565	40,920	40,920
North Dakota	1,169	1,030	1,061	13.7	16.5	18.0	16,025	15,995	18,918	1,480	1,802	1,680	18.1	22.5	21.0	26,249	35,297	35,280
South Dakota	3,887	2,677	2,772	11.7	17.5	17.0	48,802	46,848	47,124	1,696	1,845	1,845	21.9	21.0	26.0	39,588	43,929	47,970
Nebraska	8,796	6,014	6,072	16.0	12.0	17.0	149,599	82,032	102,288	2,061	1,419	1,481	21.8	14.5	22.0	45,261	20,576	31,482
Kansas	4,998	2,787	2,772	12.7	13.5	18.0	67,788	37,220	49,896	1,467	1,366	1,610	22.3	15.5	25.5	32,822	21,173	41,055
Delaware	142	144	141	27.5	29.0	28.0	4,176	4,176	3,948	3	3	3	30.2	29.0	31.0	91	87	93
Maryland	510	506	511	31.2	36.0	30.0	15,923	18,216	17,374	48	41	35	28.4	27.5	29.0	1,344	1,128	1,015
Virginia	1,467	1,405	1,377	22.0	26.0	25.0	32,285	36,530	34,425	112	80	84	19.5	20.0	21.5	2,197	1,600	1,806
West Virginia	500	491	486	24.7	28.5	27.0	12,448	13,994	13,122	106	73	66	19.7	20.0	21.0	2,089	5,692	1,386
North Carolina	2,330	2,466	2,441	16.2	19.5	20.0	42,517	48,087	48,820	220	253	250	19.2	22.1	21.0	4,226	5,592	5,250
South Carolina	1,658	1,764	1,789	13.5	14.5	14.5	22,306	25,433	25,940	418	490	485	21.3	23.5	22.0	8,910	11,515	10,670
Georgia	4,107	4,346	4,172	10.1	9.2	14.5	41,328	39,941	47,978	358	426	443	19.0	21.0	19.5	6,842	8,946	8,638
Florida	743	805	821	9.2	7.5	10.5	6,871	6,038	8,620	8	9	9	14.6	15.5	14.0	114	124	126
Kentucky	2,881	2,816	2,816	23.5	25.0	25.0	64,064	70,400	70,400	121	56	63	16.2	17.0	19.0	1,969	952	1,197
Tennessee	2,872	2,685	2,740	21.5	20.0	25.0	61,741	52,700	68,500	98	85	80	16.3	17.0	19.0	1,598	1,445	1,520
Alabama	3,720	3,408	3,442	12.8	10.0	14.0	41,253	34,080	48,188	109	132	158	19.0	21.5	20.0	2,126	2,838	3,160
Mississippi	2,976	2,839	3,009	15.0	12.5	16.5	38,526	35,488	49,648	45	76	114	23.2	36.0	22.0	1,043	2,736	2,508
Arkansas	2,100	2,085	2,022	14.4	17.0	17.0	30,245	32,318	34,374	188	132	146	19.0	22.0	21.5	2,663	2,904	3,118
Louisiana	1,443	1,555	1,508	14.5	15.0	17.0	20,908	23,325	25,636	32	52	60	24.4	32.0	34.0	814	1,664	2,040
Oklahoma	2,481	1,877	1,877	15.2	14.0	19.0	33,165	27,215	35,663	1,242	1,403	1,242	20.3	17.0	21.0	25,879	21,114	29,453
Texas	4,898	4,366	4,953	15.4	16.0	18.5	75,550	73,376	91,630	1,242	1,200	1,375	23.8	23.0	25.0	35,299	28,750	34,375
Montana	137	136	146	9.5	13.0	14.0	1,345	1,768	2,044	256	291	279	22.1	27.5	26.0	5,716	8,002	7,254
Idaho	35	32	31	35.1	34.0	37.0	1,231	1,138	1,147	156	164	157	29.6	36.0	35.0	4,827	6,232	5,652
Wyoming	203	161	169	10.2	11.0	11.5	2,107	1,771	1,944	101	115	88	24.3	26.0	23.5	2,762	2,288	2,070
Colorado	1,382	766	835	10.4	10.5	10.0	14,838	8,043	8,350	160	145	145	27.8	29.0	27.5	4,460	4,205	3,988
New Mexico	207	189	178	13.6	15.0	14.0	2,847	2,552	2,492	25	29	29	23.4	22.0	22.0	581	638	638
Arizona	32	28	29	15.2	12.5	17.0	494	275	494	10	10	10	26.9	23.0	27.0	285	230	270
Utah	19	19	20	24.6	25.0	25.0	468	475	500	37	37	28	26.1	35.0	35.0	945	980	945
Nevada	2	2	2	26.7	30.0	28.0	50	60	112	3	7	7	35.2	35.0	38.0	115	245	266
Washington	33	32	29	34.4	34.5	35.0	1,148	1,104	1,044	162	229	240	48.1	49.0	47.0	7,791	11,221	11,280
Oregon	52	51	55	35.2	31.0	31.0	1,862	1,591	1,705	275	350	340	31.5	33.5	31.0	8,682	11,725	10,540
California	73	60	63	32.6	34.0	34.0	2,368	2,040	2,142	110	136	150	26.8	29.0	29.0	3,017	3,944	4,350
United States	98,986	88,803	86,306	23.2	29.5	28.0	2,299,342	2,619,137	2,415,998	37,005	33,070	34,585	27.4	28.3	29.8	1,024,852	937,215	1,031,622

Indicated Yield and Production of Crops July 1, 1940, With Comparisons—Continued

State	Winter wheat Acreage Harvested Avg. 1929-38	1939	For harvest 1940	Yield Avg. 1929-38	1939	Ind. July 1, 1940	Prod. Avg. 1929-38	1939	Ind. July 1, 1940	Spring wheat Acreage Harvested Avg. 1929-38	1939	For harvest 1940	Yield Avg. 1929-38	1939	Ind. July 1, 1940	Prod. Avg. 1929-38	1939	Ind. July 1, 1940
	1,000 acres	1,000 acres	1,000 acres	Bush.	Bush.	Bush.	1,000 bu.	1,000 bu.	1,000 bu.	1,000 acres	1,000 acres	1,000 acres	Bush.	Bush.	Bush.	1,000 bu.	1,000 bu.	1,000 bu.
Maine										5	4	4	20.4	21.0	20.0	84	84	80
New York	231	267	264	21.0	23.5	24.5	5,317	6,274	7,203	8	6	4	16.8	18.0	17.0	137	108	85
New Jersey	56	52	55	22.0	22.5	23.0	1,226	1,170	1,288									
Pennsylvania	977	916	916	19.4	21.0	20.5	19,033	19,236	18,778	11	10	11	17.8	18.5	19.0	204	185	209
Ohio	1,994	1,901	1,939	20.1	19.5	20.0	40,043	37,070	38,780	10	5	5	17.4	16.0	19.0	170	80	95
Indiana	1,732	1,525	1,540	17.4	18.0	18.0	30,188	27,450	27,720	11	9	6	15.4	16.0	16.0	182	162	96
Illinois	2,018	1,829	1,755	17.4	21.0	19.0	35,180	38,409	33,345	69	36	26	16.3	17.0	18.0	1,207	612	468
Michigan	816	720	740	20.4	21.0	22.0	16,460	15,120	16,478	18	19	18	15.9	16.0	16.0	283	304	288
Wisconsin	36	40	40	17.7	15.0	18.5	633	600	740	74	50	46	16.5	15.0	17.0	1,211	750	782
Minnesota	175	144	153	18.4	17.5	19.5	3,247	2,520	2,984	1,389	1,390	1,518	12.8	13.5	14.0	17,748	18,630	21,252
Iowa	288	350	236	18.0	17.0	18.5	7,009	5,950	4,216	36	40	30	13.8	13.5	14.5	510	540	435
Missouri	1,837	1,770	1,770	13.7	15.5	16.0	25,457	26,205	28,320	8	8	1	12.4	12.0	12.0	104	36	12
North Dakota										5,546	5,347	5,750	7.5	10.5	9.5	44,285	56,144	54,625
South Dakota	117	96	100	11.4	9.5	8.0	1,381	912	900	1,728	1,692	1,887	7.5	7.7	8.0	14,799	13,028	15,096
Nebraska	2,997	3,081	2,525	14.0	11.5	10.5	42,867	35,432	26,523	276	118	135	8.6	8.0	6.0	2,214	944	810
Kansas	11,047	9,706	7,785	11.9	11.5	11.5	135,801	111,619	89,298	19	7	25	7.8	5.5	6.0	170	38	150
Delaware	89	72	74	17.6	18.0	18.0	1,568	1,296	1,332									
Maryland	445	377	392	19.1	16.5	19.0	8,518	7,352	7,448									
Virginia	613	518	539	14.2	14.5	14.5	8,735	7,511	8,354									
West Virginia	139	145	137	14.9	14.5	14.5	2,080	2,102	1,986									
North Carolina	435	425	446	10.7	12.0	13.0	4,651	5,100	5,798									
South Carolina	123	210	210	9.8	11.5	12.5	1,175	2,415	2,625									
Georgia	130	177	181	9.0	10.0	10.0	1,134	1,770	1,810									
Kentucky	376	354	375	14.1	11.5	15.0	5,366	4,075	5,625									
Tennessee	388	358	379	11.0	11.5	12.5	4,241	4,117	4,738									
Alabama	5	6	6	10.2	12.0	12.5	54	72	75									
Arkansas	59	41	34	9.1	9.5	9.5	534	390	323									
Oklahoma	4,048	4,317	3,885	11.4	14.0	14.0	46,763	60,438	54,390									
Texas	3,152	2,765	2,627	10.0	10.0	10.0	33,958	27,650	26,270									
Montana	669	1,099	1,193	13.6	20.0	17.0	9,669	21,980	20,281	2,673	2,565	2,895	5.8	13.5	12.5	24,586	34,628	36,188
Idaho	640	595	657	20.4	24.0	25.0	13,166	14,280	15,763	445	298	320	25.6	28.0	27.0	11,457		8,640
Wyoming	120	181	190	10.6	9.5	11.0	1,318	1,720	2,090	129	95	110	11.3	11.5	11.0	1,479	1,092	1,210
Colorado	741	902	748	11.6	11.0	11.0	9,003	9,922	8,228	305	170	282	12.9	13.5	13.0	3,944	2,295	3,666
New Mexico	233	274	214	9.4	10.0	9.0	2,565	2,740	1,926	26	20	21	13.4	11.0	12.5	356	220	262
Arizona	38	35	37	22.4	23.0	20.0	841	805	740									
Utah	180	186	186	16.4	14.0	16.0	3,059	2,240	2,976	76	66	65	28.0	26.5	26.0	2,145	1,749	1,890
Nevada	3	3	5	23.0	29.0	27.0	70	87	135	13	17	16	24.2	25.0	25.0	312	425	400
Washington	1,017	1,185	1,078	23.8	25.5	25.5	24,342	30,218	27,489	1,194	716	1,002	16.6	19.0	18.0	20,078	13,604	18,036
Oregon	664	630	640	19.4	22.0	21.3	12,974	13,640	13,760	307	155	250	20.5	20.5	20.5	6,312	3,178	5,125
California	682	586	750	18.1	18.0	15.0	12,489	10,648	11,250									
United States	39,453	37,802	34,923	14.3	14.9	15.0	571,067	563,431	523,990	14,381	12,828	14,428	10.6	12.3	11.8	154,000	157,180	169,700

State	Barley Acreage Harvested Avg. 1929-38	1939	For harvest 1940	Yield Avg. 1929-38	1939	Ind. July 1, 1940	Prod. Avg. 1929-38	1939	Ind. July 1, 1940	Rye Acreage Harvested Avg. 1929-38	1939	For harvest 1940	Yield Avg. 1929-38	1939	Ind. July 1, 1940	Prod. Avg. 1929-38	1939	Ind. July 1, 1940
	1,000 acres	1,000 acres	1,000 acres	Bush.	Bush.	Bush.	1,000 bu.	1,000 bu.	1,000 bu.	1,000 acres	1,000 acres	1,000 acres	Bush.	Bush.	Bush.	1,000 bu.	1,000 bu.	1,000 bu.
Maine	4	4	4	29.3	29.0	30.0	117	116	120									
Vermont	4	5	5	27.0	28.0	27.0	105	140	135									
New York	160	146	136	24.0	27.0	25.0	3,840	3,942	3,400	22	22	20	15.7	15.5	16.5	348	341	363
New Jersey	1	5	6	27.2	30.0	31.0	30	150	248	24	23	20	17.3	17.0	17.5	416	391	350
Pennsylvania	61	124	150	26.0	25.0	28.0	1,601	3,658	4,200	100	73	74	13.8	14.5	14.5	903	1,058	1,073
Ohio	55	50	55	25.2	25.0	28.0	1,278	1,250	1,540	44	85	86	13.8	14.5	14.5	903	1,232	1,247
Indiana	30	43	60	20.2	21.0	24.0	622	903	1,440	121	134	125	11.7	12.0	13.0	1,424	1,608	1,625
Illinois	281	169	135	24.8	24.5	29.5	5,855	4,140	3,982	86	88	53	12.0	12.5	13.5	1,048	1,100	716
Michigan	216	199	175	22.4	29.0	27.3	4,820	5,771	4,812	134	121	88	11.0	12.5	13.5	1,830	1,512	1,188
Wisconsin	788	779	662	27.2	29.0	30.0	21,296	22,591	19,860	244	228	202	11.1	10.0	12.5	2,768	2,380	2,526
Minnesota	1,974	2,186	2,106	21.6	26.0	25.0	43,217	56,808	50,200	418	525	383	11.2	14.0	16.0	6,533	7,350	6,128
Iowa	506	563	400	24.3	24.5	27.0	12,486	13,794	10,800	78	72	42	14.6	14.5	15.5	1,234	1,044	651
Missouri	48	163	170	17.5	21.0	19.5	852	3,423	3,315	31	42	26	11.0	10.0	10.5	381	420	368
North Dakota	1,735	1,655	1,804	14.0	18.1	17.0	25,478	30,618	30,668	271	830	677	9.3	8.5	12.0	2,865	7,106	8,124
South Dakota	1,414	1,449	1,608	15.3	17.0	18.0	24,661	24,633	28,944	356	528	391	10.8	9.0	11.0	4,555	4,752	4,301
Nebraska	996	1,127	1,431	17.6	13.0	10.5	12,831	14,651	21,465	308	446	326	10.0	10.0	10.5	3,008	3,568	2,606
Kansas	287	680	1,008	13.7	11.0	15.0	3,691	7,480	15,090	38	65	60	10.6	10.0	10.5	407	650	630
Delaware										9	11		12.6	13.0	13.5	83	117	148
Maryland	81	72	76	29.4	30.0	28.0	904	2,160	2,128	20	32	28	12.5	12.5	12.5	248	250	252
Virginia	38	80	84	24.8	30.0	28.0	933	2,330	2,184	51	48	43	11.6	11.5	12.0	601	576	516
West Virginia	4	10	9	24.6	24.5	23.0	112	245	225	11	7	7	11.6	10.5	11.0	133	74	77
North Carolina	15	11	13	18.1	20.0	20.0	266	220	260	64	61	61	7.6	7.5	7.5	486	458	458
South Carolina										10	12	8	7.5	9.5	9.0	76	95	108
Georgia										18	21	21	6.0	6.5	6.5	104	136	136
Kentucky	18	51	64	22.4	22.0	21.0	410	1,122	1,600	19	14	17	10.9	9.0	12.0	216	126	204
Tennessee	27	55	70	17.6	17.5	19.0	471	962	1,330	29	42	44	6.9	7.0	7.5	199	294	332
Oklahoma	101	378	344	15.2	16.0	16.0	1,600	6,048	5,504	8	7	9	5.0	8.5	7.0	39	60	63
Texas	196	197	227	16.0	15.0	16.0	2,445	2,955	3,632	7	7	5	9.0	8.5	9.0	30	60	45
Montana	141	212	201	19.0	24.0	22.0	2,621	5,088	4,422	38	35	25	9.0	12.0	11.0	353	420	275
Idaho	126	155	183	33.8	36.0	34.0	4,249	5,580	6,388	6	5	8	10.7	11.0	12.0	60	55	96
Wyoming	77	65	67	31.3	24.0	24.0	1,601	1,860	1,608	25	25	27	6.6	8.0	7.0	168	200	189
Colorado	427	388	466	19.0	10.5	19.0	8,096	3,560	8,854	42	66	55	7.3	6.5	7.5	322	429	412
New Mexico	7	9	9	20.8	20.0	18.0	154	160	162									
Arizona	22	34	39	30.4	33.0	31.0	688	1,122	1,209									
Utah	45	65	70	37.6	37.0	37.0	1,712	2,405	2,580	2	4	4	7.6	8.0	7.0	20	32	28
Nevada	7	15	17	37.2	35.0	38.0	260	525	570									
Washington	56	95	139	31.6	32.5	32.0	1,791	3,120	4,448	20	26	29	8.0	10.0	11.0	136	260	319
Oregon	97	177	200	29.0	28.3	29.0	2,806	5,222	5,800	34	45	65	12.6	12.5	14.0	431	562	910
California	1,099	1,234	1,197	26.7	25.0	28.5	29,590	30,850	34,114	8	6	8	12.6	11.0	14.0	97	66	112
United States	10,795	12,600	13,290	20.6	21.9	21.6	225,486	276,298	287,377	3,250	3,811	3,086	11.4	10.3	11.9	38,095	39,249	36,848

Indicated Yield and Production of Crops July 1, 1940, With Comparisons—Continued

	Tame hay									Wild hay									Pasture		
	Acreage			Yield per acre			Production			Acreage			Yield per acre			Production			Condition July 1		
State	Harvested		For harvest, 1940	Average, 1929-38	1939	Indicated July 1, 1940	Average, 1929-38	1939	Indicated July 1, 1940	Harvested		For harvest, 1940	Average, 1929-38	1939	Indicated July 1, 1940	Average, 1929-38	1939	Indicated July 1, 1940	Average, 1929-38	1939	1940
	Average, 1929-38	1939								Average, 1929-38	1939										
	1,000 acres	1,000 acres	1,000 acres	Tons	Tons	Tons	1,000 tons	1,000 tons	1,000 tons	1,000 acres	1,000 acres	1,000 acres	Tons	Tons	Tons	1,000 tons	1,000 tons	1,000 tons	Pct.	Pct.	Pct.
Maine	989	1,005	1,005	0.87	0.91	0.90	862	918	904	7	7	7	0.93	0.95	0.95	6	7	7	86	84	90
N. H.	374	388	388	1.02	1.02	1.08	380	394	419	8	7	8	.90	.90	.90	6	7	6	85	83	91
Vt.	927	933	936	1.17	1.21	1.25	1,085	1,133	1,170	8	10	10	.90	1.00	1.00	7	10	10	87	93	96
Mass.	365	396	399	1.34	1.27	1.45	488	504	579	8	8	7	.93	.95	1.00	7	8	7	84	73	91
R. I.	40	45	46	1.24	1.16	1.30	50	52	60	1	1	1	.85	.85	.90	1	1	1	85	69	90
Conn.	308	343	343	1.32	1.20	1.40	408	412	480	8	10	9	1.08	1.10	1.15	9	11	10	87	66	95
N. Y.	4,059	3,962	3,948	1.22	1.05	1.40	4,949	4,179	5,527	44	58	88	.90	.85	1.00	40	49	58	80	71	96
N. J.	222	219	223	1.51	1.37	1.70	334	299	379	13	12	11	1.24	1.30	1.35	17	16	15	79	59	86
Pa.	2,478	2,406	2,410	1.20	1.10	1.45	2,968	2,658	3,494	13	14	14	.79	.70	.90	10	10	13	78	71	92
Ohio	2,612	2,720	2,551	1.14	1.32	1.50	2,979	3,577	4,276	4	5	5	.72	.85	.90	3	4	4	73	84	96
Ind.	1,874	1,969	2,267	1.14	1.38	1.40	2,138	2,723	3,174	8	6	6	.88	.90	1.00	7	5	6	73	88	94
Ill.	2,714	2,877	3,246	1.21	1.45	1.35	3,279	4,183	4,382	19	12	14	.82	.80	.90	16	10	13	74	91	86
Mich.	2,585	2,640	2,677	1.20	1.29	1.55	3,096	3,415	4,149	35	28	22	.81	.85	.90	28	24	20	77	88	96
Wis.	3,261	3,980	4,021	1.41	1.46	1.75	4,645	5,829	7,037	284	250	250	.98	1.05	1.00	272	262	250	78	88	98
Minn.	2,662	3,075	3,134	1.33	1.55	1.50	3,548	4,773	4,701	1,678	1,257	1,315	.90	1.00	.95	1,514	1,357	1,250	75	85	83
Iowa	3,115	3,498	4,071	1.36	1.38	1.50	4,216	4,814	6,106	179	135	136	.98	1.05	1.00	175	142	136	78	82	82
Mo.	2,750	2,954	3,158	.88	1.09	1.05	2,427	3,222	3,315	135	115	135	.94	1.20	1.10	128	138	145	70	91	82
N. Dak.	1,214	1,044	1,001	.90	1.05	1.10	1,079	865	1,101	1,529	1,282	1,295	.71	.75	.85	1,120	962	1,101	61	74	75
S. Dak.	1,024	775	738	.84	.93	.90	865	719	664	1,636	1,636	1,731	.52	.55	.55	909	900	945	62	60	73
Nebr.	1,528	909	951	1.38	1.23	1.30	2,103	1,118	1,236	2,550	2,193	2,193	.63	.60	.55	1,644	1,316	1,206	71	69	59
Kans.	1,058	739	887	1.35	1.35	1.40	1,443	994	1,330	799	655	655	.85	1.00	1.00	690	655	655	68	72	70
Del.	62	72	74	1.31	1.26	1.40	82	91	104	1	1	1	1.05	1.00	1.20	2	1	1	78	66	86
Md.	383	413	422	1.21	1.25	1.40	464	518	591	4	†4	4	.86	1.00	1.00	3	4	4	76	77	80
Va.	963	1,036	1,071	.95	.95	1.10	923	983	1,178	10	16	18	.76	.85	.85	7	14	14	78	72	90
W. Va.	672	708	713	.96	1.01	1.15	644	718	820	10	13	12	.76	.85	.90	7	10	11	74	76	89
N. C.	859	1,107	1,190	.81	.90	.87	698	991	1,035	25	40	40	.95	1.10	1.00	24	44	40	75	79	82
Ga.	498	655	690	.72	.85	.75	362	541	518	17	25	25	.76	.75	.80	13	19	20	67	68	75
Fla.	833	1,111	1,135	.54	.52	.57	450	579	647	19	20	19	.78	.80	.80	15	15	15	68	83	80
Ky.	90	100	103	.55	.51	.55	49	51	57	2	1	1	.68	.65	.65	2	1	1	77	84	81
Tenn.	1,285	1,367	1,428	1.01	1.16	1.30	1,317	1,582	1,714	19	25	25	.90	1.10	1.00	16	28	25	73	90	89
Ala.	1,598	1,621	1,632	.91	1.00	.95	1,372	1,629	1,541	35	47	42	.73	.95	.80	26	45	34	69	87	77
Miss.	673	840	843	.73	.71	.75	494	596	632	41	40	40	.80	.80	.85	33	34	34	68	90	81
Ark.	600	897	904	1.17	1.27	1.20	708	1,140	1,085	60	85	70	.95	1.20	1.05	59	102	74	70	88	80
La.	749	991	1,045	1.09	1.09	1.00	746	1,080	1,046	160	143	143	.94	1.15	1.05	150	164	150	71	88	82
Okla.	257	321	328	1.18	1.26	1.25	300	406	410	21	19	20	1.00	1.30	1.30	21	25	26	70	81	82
Tex.	532	626	629	1.26	1.21	1.35	668	755	849	499	478	478	.85	1.00	1.00	424	478	478	67	77	77
Mont.	774	1,163	1,166	.97	.88	1.10	745	1,022	1,283	242	271	285	.90	.95	.95	220	257	271	70	69	81
Idaho	1,479	1,293	1,286	1.17	1.47	1.50	1,724	1,900	1,929	551	523	523	.76	1.00	.90	400	551	471	70	89	89
Wyo.	1,051	1,040	1,020	2.13	2.11	2.35	2,239	2,198	2,397	90	81	81	.95	.90	.90	86	73	81	89	82	86
Colo.	745	732	749	1.20	1.10	1.30	892	803	970	280	269	274	.68	.70	.70	196	161	192	82	74	85
N. Mex.	4,140	1,037	1,040	1.57	1.48	1.55	1,797	1,537	1,612	356	344	354	.92	.80	.95	332	275	336	73	61	67
Ariz.	133	138	139	2.00	1.96	2.00	265	265	278	23	24	25	.74	.55	.70	17	13	18	67	61	71
Utah	196	218	223	2.59	2.13	2.25	509	475	502	11	7	8	.98	.80	1.00	10	6	8	80	73	76
Nev.	526	507	500	2.00	1.91	2.06	1,056	968	1,030	63	60	58	1.00	1.05	1.05	66	60	61	75	69	68
Wash.	190	184	187	1.91	1.84	2.05	363	338	383	122	137	137	.98	.90	1.00	122	128	137	81	84	89
Oreg.	916	989	1,010	1.79	1.81	2.05	1,633	1,891	2,070	30	28	28	1.18	1.30	1.20	36	34	34	82	80	82
Calif.	882	324	816	1.76	1.79	1.85	1,476	1,510	1,309	228	209	215	1.00	1.00	1.06	227	209	239	84	74	81
	1,653	1,484	1,542	2.59	2.82	3.00	4,259	4,184	4,626	149	159	184	1.10	1.00	1.30	167	159	239	75	64	86
United States	55,808	58,347	60,573	1.25	1.30	1.41	69,650	75,726	85,301	12,019	10,898	10,973	.76	.81	.81	9,298	8,800	8,862	73	78	83

	Flaxseed									Beans, dry edible [1]								
	Acreage			Yield per acre			Production			Acreage			Yield per acre			Production		
State	Harvested		For harvest, 1940	Average, 1929-38	1939	Indicated July 1, 1940	Average, 1929-38	1939	Indicated July 1, 1940	Harvested		For harvest, 1940	Average, 1929-38	1939	Indicated July 1, 1940	Average, 1929-38	1939	Indicated July 1, 1940
	Average, 1929-38	1939								Average, 1929-38	1939							
	1,000 acres	1,000 acres	1,000 acres	Bushels	Bushels	Bushels	1,000 bushels	1,000 bushels	1,000 bushels	1,000 acres	1,000 acres	1,000 acres	Pounds	Pounds	Pounds	1,000 bags [2]	1,000 bags [2]	1,000 bags [2]
Maine										8	11	10	855	910	830	70	100	82
Vermont										3	3	3	600	640	640	19	18	19
New York										140	140	151	785	810	730	1,062	1,134	1,087
Michigan	7	9	9	8.8	8.5	7.5	68	68	68	561	482	520	725	825	730	3,974	4,520	3,796
Wisconsin	5	11	14	10.7	11.0	11.0	59	121	154	6	2	2	388	430	410	21	9	8
Minnesota	641	1,223	1,541	8.2	10.0	10.0	5,140	12,230	15,410	5	2	2	312	450	250	16	9	5
Iowa	17	90	200	9.1	10.5	12.0	147	945	2,400									
Missouri	3	4		4.2	6.5	6.0	13	26	30									
North Dakota	755	411	658	4.3	5.0	5.5	3,342	2,055	3,619									
South Dakota	215	162	282	4.2	8.0	7.5	959	1,296	2,115									
Nebraska	7	6		5.6	6.0		88	8	14	14	14	9	715	1,100	950	104	154	180
Kansas	48	98	130	5.9	7.9	8.0	280	735	1,040	4		1	[3] 262		275	29		3
Texas		18	29		11.5	6.0		207	174									
Idaho	144	125	135	3.6	4.5	5.0	495	562	675	26	15	17	1,091	1,380	1,250	274	207	212
Wyoming		10	5		8.0	8.0		85	40	120	110	130	1,282	1,410	1,400	1,522	1,551	1,820
Colorado										88	46	50	1,052	1,000	1,100	408	460	550
New Mexico										320	272	313	336	500	380	1,118	1,300	1,189
Arizona		5	12	22.0	22.0		110	264		153	146	162	342	280	350	542	409	567
Washington		7	9		10.0	10.0		99	70		10	11	468	230	550	41	22	60
Oregon		5			9.5	9.8		57	48	2	2	2	616	900	800	12	18	16
California	[3] 33	108	134	[3] 17.3	16.0	20.0	[3] 549	1,728	2,680	5	329	338	1,187	1,213	1,261	3,879	3,990	4,516
United States	1,868	2,284	3,168	5.0	8.9	9.1	10,846	20,330	28,901	1,737	1,554	1,751	769.0	898.5	805.9	13,086	13,962	14,111

[1] Includes beans grown for seed. [2] Bags of 100 pounds. [3] Short-time average.

Indicated Yield and Production of Crops July 1, 1940, With Comparisons—Continued

State	Clover & timothy hay[1] Acreage Harv. Avg 1929-38	1939	For harvest 1940	Yield Avg 1929-38	1939	Indic. July 1, 1940	Prod. Avg 1929-38	1939	Indic. July 1, 1940	Alfalfa hay[1] Acreage Harv. Avg 1929-38	1939	For harvest 1940	Yield Avg 1929-38	1939	Indic. July 1, 1940	Prod. Avg 1929-38	1939	Indic. July 1, 1940	Soybeans Acreage alone Avg 1929-38	1939	1940	Cowpeas Acreage alone Avg 1929-38	1939	1940
	1,000 acres	1,000 acres	1,000 acres	Tons	Tons	Tons	1,000 tons	1,000 tons	1,000 tons	1,000 acres	1,000 acres	1,000 acres	Tons	Tons	Tons	1,000 tons	1,000 tons	1,000 tons	1,000 acres	1,000 acres	1,000 acres	1,000 acres	1,000 acres	1,000 acres
Maine	546	475	480	0.97	1.02	1.00	532	484	480	6	6	6	1.48	1.45	1.50	9	9							
N.H.	207	216	218	1.15	1.10	1.25	238	238	272	3	3	3	1.97	1.60	2.10	7	5	6						
Vt.	697	684	684	1.21	1.25	1.30	846	855	889	11	13	14	2.20	1.95	2.50	24	25	33						
Mass.	258	289	262	1.44	1.32	1.45	373	381	453	6	8	9	2.26	2.15	2.40	14	17	22						
R.I.	22	25	26	1.36	1.25	1.45	30	31	38	1	1	1	2.28	2.20	2.45	2	2	2						
Conn.	165	191	191	1.40	1.25	1.50	232	239	266	12	16	15	2.78	2.30	3.05	35	37	46						
N.Y.	3,248	3,002	2,942	1.21	1.05	1.40	3,928	3,152	4,119	267	292	321	1.89	1.55	2.10	505	453	674	6	9	13			
N.J.	151	117	115	1.36	1.10	1.50	206	129	172	39	48	52	2.16	2.00	2.45	85	96	127	4	30	35			
Pa.	2,180	2,025	2,005	1.16	1.05	1.40	2,518	2,126	2,807	159	215	226	1.89	1.65	2.15	304	355	486	26	69	80	1	1	1
Ohio	2,018	1,755	1,843	1.02	1.10	1.30	2,049	1,930	2,396	351	516	537	1.82	2.00	2.20	653	1,032	1,181	241	823	1,070	3	4	4
Ind.	1,093	785	1,060	0.97	1.10	1.25	1,055	864	1,325	310	474	474	1.69	1.80	2.00	525	853	948	629	1,377	1,460	33	40	44
Ill.	1,248	1,028	1,384	1.06	1.20	1.30	1,366	1,230	1,799	351	471	476	2.04	2.25	2.30	707	1,060	1,095	1,394	2,726	2,944	190	214	300
Mich.	1,494	1,291	1,265	1.04	1.15	1.20	1,549	1,485	1,644	573	1,109	1,144	1.53	1.60	1.90	1,342	1,650	2,174	32	148	225			
Wis.	2,105	2,328	2,351	1.27	1.35	1.55	2,753	3,143	3,644	681	1,127	1,150	1.96	1.75	2.40	1,343	1,972	2,760	126	249	311			
Minn.	946	886	859	1.21	1.35	1.30	1,146	1,196	1,117	877	1,212	1,260	1.72	2.00	2.00	1,553	2,424	2,520		171	231			
Iowa	1,820	1,871	1,917	1.12	1.05	1.05	2,072	1,650	2,896	708	879	914	2.07	2.10	2.20	1,440	1,846	2,011	510	1,160	1,220			
Mo.	1,753	1,210	1,210	0.78	0.90	0.95	1,370	1,089	1,150	181	210	214	1.90	2.25	2.30	341	472	492	408	390	421	90	80	100
N.Dak.	28	16	12	0.90	1.00	1.10	25	16	13	196	114	112	1.02	1.10	1.35	206	125	151						
S.Dak.	34	16	15	0.77	0.85	0.95	27	14	14	531	341	222	0.94	0.95	1.05	518	229	233						
Nebr.	60	15	12	0.97	0.95	1.00	62	12	12	1,096	608	678	1.51	1.30	1.40	1,670	790	509	5	12	21			
Kans.	111	33	40	0.94	1.05	1.10	110	33	42	690	410	488	1.52	1.60	1.70	1,042	656	830	37	50	60	5	11	12
Del.	40	36	39	1.20	1.15	1.40	48	43	55	6	3	5	2.32	2.30	2.50	13	12	15	30	43	45	2	2	2
Md.	300	303	303	1.12	1.20	1.35	339	364	409	30	35	36	1.95	1.85	2.20	59	65	79	36	50	55	8	9	10
Va.	460	438	438	1.00	0.90	1.20	467	394	526	53	65	62	1.72	1.85	2.00	91	120	124	104	110	110	88	70	80
W.Va.	445	382	378	0.95	1.00	1.15	420	382	435	16	27	30	1.76	2.00	2.10	30	54	63	39	52	54	2	2	2
N.C.	65	76	79	0.90	1.00	0.95	60	76	75	7	9	10	1.82	1.60	1.75	12	14	18	228	306	337	150	142	139
S.C.										3	2	2	1.71	1.55	1.65	5	3	5	19	35	32	305	350	368
Ga.	4	4	4	0.96	0.95	0.95	3	4	4	5	6	6	1.78	1.60	1.90	9	9	11	58	85	85	253	267	267
Fla.																						24	22	23
Ky.	405	350	371	0.92	1.10	1.15	382	385	427	127	176	185	1.56	1.80	1.80	202	317	333	116	143	172	63	50	55
Tenn.	264	225	214	0.91	0.95	1.00	243	214	214	38	72	75	1.62	1.70	1.80	62	122	135	162	187	165	195	111	128
Ala.	5	5	5	0.81	0.95	0.95	4	5	5	3	4	5	1.30	1.40	1.35	4	4	7	173	230	235	167	183	183
Miss.	4	8	9	1.24	1.30	1.30	5	10	12	43	65	67	2.30	2.30	2.25	96	150	151	173	276	304	153	203	189
Ark.	57	52	42	.88	1.00	.85	51	52	36	64	82	90	1.87	1.80	1.85	120	148	166	121	190	171	292	331	301
La.										17	22	24	2.08	2.20	2.00	36	48	48	36	78	84	90	96	86
Okla.										231	264	259	1.76	1.65	1.95	404	436	505	15	18	14	78	102	100
Tex.										68	108	113	2.27	2.20	2.40	154	248	271	[2]34	38	32	326	637	643
Mont.	231	236	224	1.27	1.30	1.60	295	307	358	679	662	695	1.55	1.80	1.80	1,057	1,192	1,251						
Idaho	141	140	133	1.36	1.30	1.45	193	182	193	780	773	758	2.42	2.40	2.70	1,892	1,855	2,047						
Wyo.	106	103	103	1.08	1.15	1.14	114	98	118	367	371	371	1.45	1.45	1.55	554	537	575						
Colo.	184	142	135	1.87	1.10	1.40	211	156	189	604	641	622	1.89	1.85	1.98	1,314	1,186	1,231						
N.Mex.	8	7	8	1.27	1.15	1.25	10	8	10	90	91	93	2.37	2.40	2.45	214	218	228						
Ariz.										152	156	161	2.90	2.50	2.60	443	390	419						
Utah	22	20	22	1.45	1.25	1.55	32	25	34	479	447	447	2.05	2.00	2.15	994	894	961						
Nev.	24	21	21	1.27	1.10	1.40	31	23	29	138	136	139	2.17	2.10	2.30	301	286	320						
Wash.	189	204	204	2.06	2.15	2.20	389	439	449	229	300	318	2.52	2.40	2.70	577	720	859						
Oreg.	114	85	80	1.58	1.45	1.65	180	123	132	255	264	269	2.50	2.55	2.60	636	673	699						
Calif.	37	35	35	1.62	1.60	1.80	60	56	63	750	751	781	4.02	4.30	4.40	2,997	3,229	3,436						
U.S.	23,263	20,828	21,768	1.12	1.14	1.32	26,030	23,640	28,840	12,678	13,494	13,838	1.94	2.00	2.20	24,597	27,035	30,490	4,756	9,023	10,286	2,476	2,923	3,059

State	Rice Acreage Harv. Avg 1929-38	1939	For harvest 1940	Yield Avg 1929-38	1939	Indic. July 1, 1940	Prod. Avg 1929-38	1939	Indic. July 1, 1940	Sugarcane for sirup Acreage Harv. Avg 1929-38	1939	For harvest 1940	Velvetbeans Acreage alone Avg 1929-38	1939	1940
	1,000 acres	1,000 acres	1,000 acres	Bushels	Bushels	Bushels	1,000 bushels	1,000 bushels	1,000 bushels	1,000 acres	1,000 acres	1,000 acres	1,000 acres	1,000 acres	1,000 acres
South Carolina										5	5	4	12	25	28
Georgia										33	34	27	44	71	75
Florida										12	12	11	9	8	8
Alabama										24	28	21	25	32	30
Mississippi										25	27	19	12	17	18
Arkansas	163	171	197	50.7	51.0	52.0	8,320	8,721	10,244	1	1	1			
Louisiana	454	479	489	40.3	43.0	41.0	18,316	20,597	20,049	25	32	35	6	8	8
Texas	191	269	291	51.0	52.0	54.0	9,770	13,988	15,714	9	6	5			
California	115	120	118	68.2	75.0	70.0	7,848	9,000	8,260						
United States	924	1,039	1,095	47.9	50.3	49.6	44,254	52,305	54,267	133	145	123	107	151	167

[1] Included in tame hay. Clover and timothy hay excludes sweetclover and lespedeza.   [2] Short-time average.

Indicated Yield and Production of Crops July 1, 1940, With Comparisons—Continued

Potatoes[1]

Group and State	Acreage — Harvested Average, 1929-38	Acreage — Harvested 1939	Acreage For harvest, 1940	Yield per acre Average, 1929-38	Yield per acre 1939	Yield per acre Indicated July 1, 1940	Production Average, 1929-38	Production 1939	Production Indicated July 1, 1940
	1,000 acres	*1,000 acres*	*1,000 acres*	*Bushels*	*Bushels*	*Bushels*	*1,000 bu.*	*1,000 bu.*	*1,000 bu.*
Surplus late potato States:									
Maine	168	170	177	269	225	255	45,137	38,250	45,135
New York	233	211	215	123	127	122	28,811	26,797	26,230
Pennsylvania	210	187	191	119	120	118	24,927	22,440	22,538
3 Eastern	611	568	583	161.7	154.0	161.1	98,875	87,487	93,903
Michigan	278	250	250	92	97	95	25,778	24,250	23,750
Wisconsin	258	197	197	86	88	85	22,208	17,336	16,745
Minnesota	316	289	249	75	85	80	23,830	20,315	19,920
North Dakota	130	165	177	70	⁵ 85	80	9,137	14,025	14,160
South Dakota	45	30	32	53	80	70	2,480	2,400	2,240
5 Central	1,028	881	905	81.1	88.9	84.9	83,222	78,326	76,815
Nebraska	104	81	82	78	⁵ 120	80	7,997	9,720	6,560
Montana	20	17	17	90	90	95	1,808	1,590	1,615
Idaho	110	⁵ 124	124	220	230	240	24,232	28,500	29,760
Wyoming	27	20	19	83	80	90	2,201	1,600	1,710
Colorado	99	90	84	144	160	125	14,178	14,400	10,500
Utah	13.2	12.6	13.0	154	160	140	2,023	2,016	1,820
Nevada	2.7	2.0	2.3	144	140	165	384	280	380
Washington	50	42	42	169	175	175	8,368	7,350	7,350
Oregon	44	45	46	146	160	165	6,378	7,200	7,590
California ⁴	29.0	40.7	41.5	233	284	275	6,813	11,559	11,412
10 Western	498.2	474.3	470.8	150.1	177.5	167.2	74,384	84,175	78,697
Total 18 surplus late	2,137.3	1,923.3	1,958.8	120.3	130.0	127.3	256,482	249,988	249,415
Other late potato States:									
New Hampshire	9.4	9.3	9.7	155	150	140	1,463	1,395	1,358
Vermont	16.6	15.0	15.4	136	130	120	2,264	1,950	1,848
Massachusetts	15.3	17.0	18.7	135	155	135	2,058	2,635	2,524
Rhode Island	3.4	4.1	4.5	171	190	170	582	779	765
Connecticut	15.7	17.5	19.1	155	185	150	2,457	3,238	2,865
5 New England	60.4	62.9	67.4	146.1	158.9	138.9	8,822	9,997	9,360
West Virginia	37	32	32	80	95	100	2,925	3,040	3,200
Ohio	127	120	121	97	103	98	12,429	12,600	11,858
Indiana	62	48	51	86	95	95	5,351	4,560	4,845
Illinois	47	37	38	75	93	90	3,499	3,441	3,420
Iowa	75	56	56	77	100	90	5,789	5,600	5,040
5 Central	348	293	298	86.1	99.8	95.2	29,862	29,241	28,363
New Mexico	5.6	6.0	6.0	72	80	80	405	480	480
Arizona	2.4	2.2	2.4	82	100	100	201	220	240
2 Southwestern	8.0	8.2	8.4	75.2	85.4	85.7	607	700	720
Total 12 other late	416.2	364.1	373.8	94.6	109.7	102.8	39,291	39,938	38,443
30 late States	2,553.5	2,287.4	2,332.6	115.1	126.7	123.4	295,772	289,926	287,858
Intermediate potato States:									
New Jersey	48	55	58	167	136	156	8,004	7,480	9,048
Delaware	5.2	4.0	4.3	87	80	90	457	320	387
Maryland	30	25	26	102	95	109	3,098	2,375	2,834
Virginia	97	78	78	118	87	121	11,607	6,786	9,438
Kentucky	48	46	47	76	84	90	3,688	3,804	4,230
Missouri	56	53	52	76	88	108	4,280	4,664	5,616
Kansas	36	28	28	79	76	104	2,937	2,128	2,912
Total 7 intermediate	321.2	289.0	293.3	106.0	95.6	117.5	33,972	27,617	34,465
37 late and intermediate	2,874.7	2,576.4	2,625.9	115.0	123.3	122.7	329,744	317,543	322,323
Early potato States:									
North Carolina	79	82	81	100	100	109	7,976	8,200	8,829
South Carolina	20	28	28	117	111	114	2,424	3,108	3,192
Georgia	16	18	19	65	79	79	1,046	1,386	1,501
Florida	28	29	28	111	120	153	3,044	3,480	4,284
Tennessee	42	41	43	69	71	75	2,883	2,911	3,225
Alabama	34	45	48	84	108	87	2,860	4,860	4,176
Mississippi	15	20	20	71	71	64	1,063	1,420	1,280
Arkansas	41	39	41	74	77	93	3,008	3,003	3,813
Louisiana	40	39	37	62	54	58	2,454	2,106	2,146
Oklahoma	37	33	33	71	68	74	2,668	2,244	2,442
Texas	52	43	47	65	62	66	3,343	2,666	3,102
California ⁴	17.9	33.3	36.5	230	333	300	4,436	11,089	10,950
Total 12 early States	421.0	450.3	461.5	87.9	103.2	106.0	37,205	46,473	48,940
Total United States	3,295.7	3,026.7	3,087.4	111.5	120.3	120.3	366,949	364,016	371,263

[1] Except for California, the estimates shown for each State under a particular group cover the entire crop, whether commercial or noncommercial, early or late.
[2] Revised from December preliminary estimate.
[3] Estimates shown for California under the surplus late States do not include the early commercial crop.
[4] Estimates shown for California under the early States cover the early commercial crop only.

Indicated Yield and Production of Crops July 1, 1940, With Comparisons—Continued

State	Tobacco — Acreage Harvested Average, 1929-38	1939	For harvest 1940	Yield per acre Average, 1929-38	1939	Indicated July 1, 1940	Production Average, 1929-38	1939	Indicated July 1, 1940	Sweetpotatoes — Acreage Harvested Average, 1929-38	1939	For harvest 1940	Yield per acre Average, 1929-38	1939	Indicated July 1, 1940	Production Average, 1929-38	1939	Indicated July 1, 1940	Sorgo for sirup — Acreage Harvested Average, 1929-38	1939	For harvest 1940
	Acres	Acres	Acres	Lb.	Lb.	Lb.	1,000 lb.	1,000 lb.	1,000 lb.	1,000 acres	1,000 acres	1,000 acres	Bu.	Bu.	Bu.	1,000 bu.	1,000 bu.	1,000 bu.	1,000 acres	1,000 acres	1,000 acres
Massachusetts	6,030	6,300	6,100	1,420	1,571	1,514	8,515	9,899	9,236												
Connecticut	17,070	17,400	17,400	1,338	1,443	1,368	23,108	25,116	23,795												
New York	940	1,500	1,600	1,235	1,350	1,300	1,120	2,025	2,080												
New Jersey										15	15	15	138	155	185	2,060	2,325	2,025			
Pennsylvania	29,570	27,200	28,000	1,226	1,322	1,005	36,004	35,987	28,135												
Ohio	36,740	32,000	30,600	902	947	955	32,924	30,295	29,220										3	3	4
Indiana	13,090	13,200	11,400	799	899	875	10,498	11,868	9,976	4	3	3	104	105	115	426	315	345			
Illinois										6	6	7	86	88	85	527	528	595	2	1	1
Wisconsin	23,680	22,300	24,500	1,319	1,408	1,341	30,559	31,406	32,857												
Minnesota	890	700	800	1,125	1,200	1,150	1,036	840	920												
Iowa										3	3	3	86	90	92	245	270	276	2	3	3
Missouri	5,950	6,800	5,800	892	925	1,100	5,382	6,290	6,380	12	13	12	79	85	85	906	1,105	1,020	12	10	10
Kansas	329	600	500	832	850	875	277	510	438	5	5	5	92	80	115	424	240	345	2	2	2
Delaware										7	8	5	124	135	135	826	675	675			
Maryland	36,390	38,200	37,800	716	780	640	26,096	29,796	24,192	8	9	10	134	160	135	1,090	1,440	1,350			
Virginia	137,330	172,100	115,900	716	836	782	97,395	143,847	90,684	37	32	31	112	129	120	4,156	4,128	3,720	3	3	3
West Virginia	4,770	3,600	3,400	676	760	775	3,262	2,736	2,635												
North Carolina	635,440	864,100	509,900	781	939	913	496,101	811,675	465,650	86	77	73	96	112	104	8,163	8,624	7,592	20	12	13
South Carolina	98,100	144,000	86,000	817	925	900	81,066	133,200	77,400	61	67	66	86	102	90	5,220	6,834	5,940	7	6	5
Georgia	76,400	126,100	74,100	846	761	951	67,464	95,986	70,500	115	117	99	73	76	71	8,412	8,892	7,029	16	16	15
Florida	10,700	33,000	18,000	865	720	924	9,504	23,760	16,640	21	19	19	69	60	65	1,468	1,140	1,235			
Kentucky	409,680	384,900	346,800	782	891	849	320,407	343,100	294,484	22	24	24	84	82	90	1,835	1,968	2,160	14	12	13
Tennessee	130,450	119,000	118,200	843	917	897	109,895	109,928	106,048	57	47	50	91	79	100	5,198	3,713	5,000	20	14	16
Alabama			600		683	830		410	415	93	110	90	82	80	77	7,560	8,800	6,930	40	31	34
Mississippi										80	83	77	92	91	90	7,223	6,142	6,930	22	17	20
Arkansas										40	40	35	75	67	65	2,935	2,680	2,275	22	18	18
Louisiana										96	95	90	70	73	70	6,586	6,935	6,300			
Oklahoma										18	21	19	65	45	80	1,213	945	1,520	4	2	3
Texas										64	63	54	72	60	77	4,690	3,780	4,158	28	30	30
California										11	10	12	105	120	115	1,164	1,200	1,380			
United States	1,673,750	2,014,500	1,437,300	815.6	917.7	898.7	1,360,661	1,848,654	1,291,685	860	862	797	84.6	84.3	86.3	72,436	72,679	68,800	216	180	190

¹ Short-time average.

Tobacco by Class and Type

Class and type	Type No.	Acreage Harvested Average, 1929-38	1939	For harvest, 1940	Yield per acre Average, 1929-38	1939	Indicated July 1, 1940	Production Average, 1929-38	1939	Indicated July 1, 1940
		Acres	Acres	Acres	Pounds	Pounds	Pounds	1,000 pounds	1,000 pounds	1,000 pounds
Flue-cured:										
Virginia	11	97,050	134,000	78,000	674	800	750	64,836	107,200	58,500
North Carolina	11	244,700	334,000	204,000	737	860	860	180,742	287,240	175,440
Total Old Belt	11	341,750	468,000	282,000	719	843	830	245,578	394,440	233,940
Eastern North Carolina Belt	12	326,100	427,000	243,000	799	990	950	259,278	422,730	230,850
North Carolina	13	57,660	94,000	55,000	862	990	950	50,295	93,060	52,250
South Carolina	13	98,100	144,000	86,000	817	925	900	81,068	133,200	77,400
Total South Carolina Belt	13	155,760	238,000	141,000	834	951	920	131,363	226,260	129,650
Georgia	14	75,580	125,000	73,000	844	760	950	65,542	95,000	69,350
Florida	14	7,990	29,500	14,000	790	700	900	6,675	20,650	12,600
Alabama	14			400			850		240	355
Total Georgia and Florida Belt	14	83,570	154,900	87,300	838	748	942	73,258	115,890	82,205
Total flue-cured	11-14	907,180	1,287,900	753,300	780	900	898	709,466	1,159,320	676,645
Fire-cured:										
Virginia	21	27,390	23,000	23,700	750	910	770	20,426	20,930	18,249
Kentucky	22	37,250	18,000	18,500	778	800	825	29,172	14,400	15,262
Tennessee	22	59,210	44,000	46,000	826	865	850	48,948	38,060	39,100
Total Clarksville and Hopkinsville	22	96,460	62,000	64,500	808	846	843	78,120	52,460	54,362
Kentucky	23	32,260	20,600	21,600	770	830	825	24,876	17,098	17,822
Tennessee	23	7,920	5,300	5,600	815	840	840	6,496	4,452	4,704
Total Paducah	23	40,180	25,900	27,200	779	832	828	31,372	21,550	22,524
Henderson Stemming (Ky.)	24	5,690	800	800	808	830	840	4,553	664	672
Total fire-cured	21-24	169,720	111,700	116,200	793	856	825	134,470	95,604	95,807

Indicated Yield and Production of Crops July 1, 1940, With Comparisons—Continued
Tobacco by Class and Type—Continued

Class and type	Type No.	Acreage Harvested Average, 1929-38	1939	For harvest, 1940	Yield per acre Average, 1929-38	1939	Indicated July 1, 1940	Production Average, 1929-38	1939	Indicated July 1, 1940
		Acres	*Acres*	*Acres*	*Pounds*	*Pounds*	*Pounds*	*1,000 pounds*	*1,000 pounds*	*1,000 pounds*
Air-cured (light):										
Ohio	31	15,330	15,500	13,800	817	890	900	12,636	13,795	12,420
Indiana	31	11,300	12,700	10,900	791	900	875	8,968	11,430	9,538
Missouri	31	6,950	6,800	5,800	892	925	1,100	5,382	6,290	6,380
Kansas	31	329	600	500	1,832	850	875	277	510	438
Virginia	31	9,150	11,700	10,300	1,022	1,060	1,050	9,410	12,402	10,815
West Virginia	31	4,770	3,600	3,400	676	760	775	3,262	2,736	2,635
North Carolina	31	6,980	9,100	7,900	828	950	900	5,797	8,645	7,110
Kentucky	31	290,200	305,000	265,000	775	900	850	225,154	274,500	225,250
Tennessee	31	60,100	67,000	63,000	861	960	940	51,884	64,320	59,220
Alabama	31		200	200		850	800		170	160
Total Burley	31	404,050	432,200	380,800	798	913	877	322,711	394,798	333,966
Southern Maryland	32	36,390	38,200	37,800	716	780	640	26,096	29,798	24,192
Total air-cured (light)	31-32	440,440	470,400	418,600	792	903	856	348,808	424,594	358,158
Air-cured (dark):										
Indiana	35	1,690	500	500	836	875	875	1,446	438	438
Kentucky	35	19,260	20,000	20,400	816	925	875	15,795	18,500	17,850
Tennessee	35	3,220	3,600	3,600	798	880	840	2,567	3,096	3,024
Total One Sucker	35	24,170	24,100	24,500	816	914	870	19,809	22,034	21,312
Green River (Ky.)	36	25,000	20,500	20,500	828	875	880	20,856	17,938	17,630
Virginia sun-cured	37	3,730	3,400	3,900	736	975	800	2,724	3,315	3,120
Total air-cured (dark)	35-37	52,900	48,000	48,900	818	902	860	43,389	43,287	42,062
Cigar filler:										
Pennsylvania Seedleaf	41	29,390	26,900	27,700	1,225	1,320	1,000	35,645	35,508	27,700
Miami Valley (Ohio)	42-44	20,990	16,500	16,800	959	1,000	1,000	19,827	16,500	16,800
Georgia	45	380	400	400	1,016	960	1,160	407	384	464
Florida	45	540	1,000	1,000	1,042	960	1,100	593	960	1,100
Total Georgia and Florida sun-grown	45	920	1,400	1,400	1,027	960	1,117	1,000	1,344	1,564
Total cigar filler	41-45	51,400	44,800	45,900	1,116	1,191	1,004	56,556	53,352	46,064
Cigar-binder:										
Massachusetts	51	230	100	100	1,549	1,620	1,575	353	162	158
Connecticut	51	8,490	7,800	8,300	1,536	1,620	1,525	12,950	12,636	12,658
Total Connecticut Valley Broadleaf	51	8,720	7,900	8,400	1,536	1,620	1,526	13,303	12,798	12,816
Massachusetts	52	4,690	4,900	5,100	1,522	1,690	1,600	7,045	8,281	8,160
Connecticut	52	3,390	3,200	3,500	1,509	1,660	1,550	5,066	5,312	5,425
Total Connecticut Valley Havana Seed	52	8,080	8,100	8,600	1,518	1,678	1,580	12,111	13,593	13,585
New York	53	940	1,500	1,600	1,235	1,350	1,300	1,120	2,025	2,080
Pennsylvania	53	280	300	300	1,346	1,530	1,450	359	459	435
Total New York and Pennsylvania Havana Seed	53	1,220	1,800	1,900	1,263	1,380	1,324	1,479	2,484	2,515
Southern Wisconsin	54	14,430	13,000	13,600	1,336	1,400	1,350	18,910	18,200	18,360
Wisconsin	55	9,250	9,300	10,900	1,296	1,420	1,330	11,848	13,206	14,497
Minnesota	55	890	700	800	1,125	1,200	1,150	1,036	840	920
Total Northern Wisconsin	55	10,140	10,000	11,700	1,286	1,405	1,318	12,885	14,046	15,417
Total cigar binder	51-55	42,590	40,800	44,200	1,405	1,498	1,418	58,488	61,121	62,693
Cigar wrapper:										
Massachusetts	61	1,110	1,300	900	1,004	1,120	1,020	1,117	1,456	918
Connecticut	61	5,170	6,400	5,600	982	1,120	1,020	5,061	7,168	5,712
Total Connecticut Valley shade-grown	61	6,280	7,700	6,500	986	1,120	1,020	6,178	8,624	6,630
Georgia	62	490	700	700	1,043	860	980	515	602	686
Florida	62	2,170	2,500	3,000	1,009	860	980	2,236	2,150	2,940
Total Georgia and Florida shade-grown	62	2,660	3,200	3,700	1,014	860	980	2,751	2,752	3,626
Total cigar wrapper	61-62	8,960	10,900	10,200	997	1,044	1,005	8,960	11,376	10,256
Total cigar types	41-62	102,950	96,500	100,300	1,216	1,304	1,187	124,004	125,849	119,013
United States	All	1,678,750	2,014,500	1,437,300	815.6	917.7	898.7	1,360,661	1,848,654	1,291,685

[1] Short-time average.

Durum Wheat

State	Acreage Harvested Average, 1929-38	1939	For harvest, 1940	Yield per acre Average, 1929-38	1939	Indicated July 1, 1940	Production Average, 1929-38	1939	Indicated July 1, 1940
	1,000 acres	*1,000 acres*	*1,000 acres*	*Bush-els*	*Bush-els*	*Bush-els*	*1,000 bushels*	*1,000 bushels*	*1,000 bushels*
Minnesota	119	71	78	13.2	13.5	14.0	1,628	958	1,092
North Dakota	2,239	2,538	2,685	9.1	11.0	10.5	21,543	27,918	28,192
South Dakota	676	457	567	7.8	12.0	10.0	6,449	5,484	5,670
3 States	3,035	3,066	3,330	9.1	11.2	10.5	29,619	34,360	34,954

247033—40——2

Wheat Production by Classes July 1, 1940, With Comparisons, for the United States

Year	Winter Hard red	Soft red	Spring Hard red	Durum [1]	White (winter and spring)	Total
	1,000 bu.	*1,000 bu.*	*1,000 bu.*	*1,000 bu.*	*1,000 bu.*	*1,000 bu.*
Average, 1929-38	317,963	202,180	114,244	31,040	89,250	754,685
1939	307,231	203,296	129,706	35,230	79,508	754,971
1940 [2]	266,786	202,764	135,740	35,890	87,455	728,644

[1] Includes durum wheat in States for which estimates are not shown separately.
[2] Indicated July 1, 1940.

Indicated Yield and Production of Crops July 1, 1940, With Comparisons—Continued

Sugarcane for Sugar

State	Acreage Harvested Average, 1929–38	1939	For harvest 1940	Yield of cane per acre Average, 1929–38	1939	Indicated July 1, 1940	Production Average, 1929–38	1939	Indicated July 1, 1940
	1,000 acres	*1,000 acres*	*1,000 acres*	*Short tons*	*Short tons*	*Short tons*	*1,000 short tons*	*1,000 short tons*	*1,000 short tons*
					For sugar				
Louisiana	214.6	238	245	16.5	21.4	19.0	3,627	5,084	4,655
Florida	14.7	20.1	24.2	31.2	35.5	35.0	469	714	847
Total	229.3	258.1	269.2	17.4	22.5	20.4	4,096	5,798	5,502
					For seed				
Louisiana	19.6	18	18	16.6	20.5	19.0	324	369	342
Florida	.6	.8	.8	32.8	35.5	37.0	19	30	30
Total	20.2	18.8	18.8	17.0	21.2	19.8	343	399	372
					For sugar and seed				
Louisiana	234.2	256	263	16.5	21.3	19.0	3,951	5,453	4,997
Florida	15.3	20.9	25.0	31.3	35.5	35.1	488	744	877
Total	249.5	276.9	288.0	17.4	22.4	20.4	4,439	6,197	5,874

Sugar Beets

State	Acreage Harvested Average, 1929–38	1939	For harvest 1940	Yield per acre Average, 1929–38	1939	Indicated July 1, 1940	Production Average, 1929–38	1939	Indicated July 1, 1940
	1,000 acres	*1,000 acres*	*1,000 acres*	*Short tons*	*Short tons*	*Short tons*	*1,000 short tons*	*1,000 short tons*	*1,000 short tons*
Ohio	32	47	43	8.4	7.7	8.0	258	363	344
Michigan	99	120	118	7.9	8.6	7.5	792	1,033	885
Nebraska	71	99	72	12.6	11.4	11.5	897	790	828
Montana	58	74	84	12.0	12.1	12.5	700	894	1,050
Idaho	51	73	73	11.3	13.5	15.0	600	985	1,095
Wyoming	46	49	44	12.0	11.0	10.5	552	539	462
Colorado	182	145	132	12.4	10.6	10.0	2,248	1,543	1,320
Utah	48	53	49	12.5	12.9	10.0	602	683	490
California	107	166	169	13.0	16.3	13.0	1,418	2,699	2,197
Other States	98	121	129	8.9	10.3	10.4	870	1,244	1,348
United States	792	917	913	11.3	11.7	11.0	8,937	10,773	10,019

Peanuts

State	Acreage grown alone for all purposes Average, 1929–38	1939	1940	Condition July 1 Average, 1929–38	1939	1940
	1,000 acres	*1,000 acres*	*1,000 acres*	*Per-cent*	*Per-cent*	*Per-cent*
Virginia	142	166	174	80	70	86
North Carolina	246	262	275	75	79	81
Tennessee	12	8	8	70	63	77
Total (Va.-N. C. area)	400	436	457	77	79	83
South Carolina	16	20	23	67	78	80
Georgia	551	774	789	73	72	81
Florida	123	150	158	70	74	81
Alabama	337	426	447	72	70	83
Mississippi	35	40	41	72	70	73
Total (S. E. area)	1,061	1,410	1,458	73	72	81
Arkansas	53	55	55	72	74	74
Louisiana	31	37	38	71	75	71
Oklahoma	57	52	65	69	75	75
Texas	270	420	420	68	71	74
Total (S. W. area)	412	564	578	69	72	74
United States	1,872	2,410	2,493	73	73	80

Hops

State	Acreage Average, 1929–38	1939	1940	Yield per acre Average, 1929–38	1939	Indicated July 1, 1940	Production [1] Average, 1929–38	1939	Indicated July 1, 1940
	Acres	*Acres*	*Acres*	*Lb.*	*Lb.*	*Lb.*	*1,000 pounds*	*1,000 pounds*	*1,000 pounds*
Washington	4,150	4,900	6,000	1,788	1,880	1,950	7,358	9,212	11,700
Oregon	19,310	19,300	19,600	953	1,000	930	18,295	19,300	18,228
California	5,540	6,800	7,100	1,583	1,598	1,400	8,662	10,868	9,940
United States	29,000	31,000	32,700	1,184	1,270	1,219	34,310	39,380	39,868

[1] For some States in certain years, production includes some quantities not available for marketing because of economic conditions and the marketing agreement allotments.

Cotton Report as of July 1, 1940

The acreage of cotton in cultivation in the United States on July 1 is estimated by the Crop Reporting Board to be 25,077,000 acres, which is 1.6 percent more than the 24,683,000 acres in cultivation on July 1, 1939, but 28.2 percent less than the 10-year (1929–38) average. If abandonment in 1940 is equal to the 10-year (1930–39) average percentage of abandonment, an acreage of 24,616,000 is indicated for harvest in 1940. This acreage is only slightly higher than the acreage harvested in 1939, but smaller than the cotton acreage harvested in any year since 1899 except 1938 and 1939. Total plantings are well below the Agricultural Conservation Program allotments, but some farmers whose plantings are in excess of their allotments will undoubtedly remove excess acreage.

The change from 1939 in the total cotton acreage is small for the United States as a whole, and in most of the important cotton-producing States. In Georgia, Alabama, Mississippi, and Arkansas the acreage is estimated to be the same as last year. In Texas there was an increase of 1 percent; in South Carolina and Tennessee, 2 percent; in Louisiana, 3 percent; and in Oklahoma, 4 percent. An increase of 10 percent took place in North Carolina, however, where a shift from tobacco to cotton has taken place. This shift in 1940 offsets a shift from cotton to tobacco in 1939. In New Mexico, the acreage in cultivation increased by about 14 percent, and in California, by 4 percent. A substantial increase of 20 percent is shown in Arizona, largely as the result of the material increase in the acreage of long-staple, American-Egyptian cotton.

The acreage of American-Egyptian cotton increased from 41,000 in 1939 to 70,000 in 1940. For 1940, this includes a small acreage in New Mexico. The acreage of long-staple sea-island cotton increased in scattered localities throughout the Cotton Belt. The acreage in cultivation in 1940 is given at 29,800 acres, an increase of about one-half over the 1939 acreage of 19,500.

State	10-year average abandonment from natural causes, 1930–39	Acreage in cultivation July 1 Average, 1929–38	1939	1940	1940 percent of 1939
	Percent	*1,000 acres*	*1,000 acres*	*1,000 acres*	
Missouri	1.1	399	380	395	104
Virginia	1.5	67	33	31	94
North Carolina	0.9	1,179	754	829	110
South Carolina	0.7	1,630	1,248	1,273	102
Georgia	0.9	2,696	1,989	1,994	100
Florida	2.9	112	74	73	99
Tennessee	1.0	950	733	748	102
Alabama	0.8	2,821	2,100	2,100	100
Mississippi	1.0	3,433	2,662	2,662	100
Arkansas	1.5	2,922	2,187	2,187	100
Louisiana	0.9	1,584	1,154	1,189	103
Oklahoma	3.9	3,096	1,855	1,939	104
Texas	2.7	13,412	8,874	8,963	101
New Mexico	3.0	120	96	109	114
Arizona	0.3	190	189	227	120
California	0.8	293	334	347	104
All other	1.7	24	..21	..21	101
United States	1.9	34,929	24,683	25,077	101.6
Sea-island [1]			19.5	29.8	153
American-Egyptian [1]	0.6	37	41	70	171
Lower California (Old Mexico) [2]	2.4	96	104	125	120

[1] Included in State and United States totals. Sea-island grown principally in Georgia and Florida. American-Egyptian grown principally in Arizona.
[2] Not included in California figures, nor in United States total.

Estimated Crop Conditions July 1, 1940, With Comparisons

Apples

[Condition on July 1 in States Having Commercial Production]

State	Average, 1929-38	1939	1940
	Percent	Percent	Percent
Maine	64	70	72
New Hampshire	62	56	67
Vermont	64	84	66
Massachusetts	62	68	64
Rhode Island	62	45	75
Connecticut	64	63	65
New York	54	73	56
New Jersey	62	68	68
Pennsylvania	51	66	59
Ohio	41	66	53
Indiana	44	66	46
Illinois	45	60	43
Michigan	56	75	56
Wisconsin	64	73	72
Minnesota	56	65	74
Iowa	56	60	76
Missouri	46	56	42
Nebraska	50	60	65
Kansas	43	60	58
Delaware	62	75	76
Maryland	50	56	61
Virginia	46	46	53
West Virginia	45	50	53
North Carolina	47	47	49
Georgia	50	53	57
Kentucky	41	42	38
Tennessee	43	47	28
Arkansas	48	45	45
Oklahoma	41	40	38
Montana	65	79	73
Washington	72	66	72
Colorado	55	52	65
New Mexico	47	53	63
Arizona	60	65	39
Utah	67	72	71
Washington	72	72	76
Oregon	71	72	73
California	70	75	60
38 States	56	64	59

Peaches

State	Condition July 1			Production [1]		
	Average, 1929-38	1939	1940	Average, 1929-38	1939	Indicated July 1, 1940
	Percent	Percent	Percent	1,000 bu.	1,000 bu.	1,000 bu.
New Hampshire	56	57	65	18	17	17
Massachusetts	58	59	69	110	74	72
Rhode Island	64	75	97	26	12	26
Connecticut	59	69	67	104	84	114
New York	55	84	70	1,368	1,722	1,400
New Jersey	60	73	81	1,307	1,435	1,530
Pennsylvania	48	71	74	1,666	2,460	2,480
Ohio	36	64	33	788	1,212	492
Indiana	36	58	13	408	378	64
Illinois	42	64	11	1,553	1,800	204
Michigan	53	88	87	1,568	2,760	1,682
Iowa	39	76	51	79	110	81
Missouri	34	46	29	782	1,140	638
Nebraska	37	62	40	41	70	51
Kansas	30	38	44	125	154	132
Delaware	60	75	80	299	422	400
Maryland	53	68	82	371	427	450
Virginia	46	60	50	906	1,025	1,227
West Virginia	34	41	61	284	815	475
North Carolina	59	42	37	1,922	1,305	1,176
South Carolina	56	66	65	1,141	1,636	1,560
Georgia	53	55	53	5,029	3,800	3,618
Florida	58	35	77	60	33	60
Kentucky	54	33	16	517	592	243
Tennessee	41	46	12	1,209	1,470	288
Alabama	49	64	26	1,335	1,705	672
Mississippi	52	71	78	798	1,034	390
Arkansas	43	66	48	1,718	2,613	1,840
Louisiana	48	62	66	369	409	442
Oklahoma	30	38	29	526	615	434
Texas	39	63	65	1,200	1,472	1,770
Idaho	51	57	83	133	136	202
Colorado	73	76	90	1,189	1,575	1,935
New Mexico	33	41	52	71	73	88
Arizona	60	58	70	58	51	47
Utah	59	80	73	439	564	525
Nevada	56	80	64	5	6	4
Washington	61	69	89	1,070	1,210	1,494
Oregon	59	82	75	276	391	361
California, all	76	88	80	21,914	24,043	23,782
Clingstone [2]	76	88	81	14,343	15,251	15,585
Freestone [3]	75	87	78	7,571	8,792	8,197
United States	58	69	60	52,723	60,822	52,486

[1] For some States in certain years, production includes some quantities unharvested on account of market conditions.
[2] Mainly for canning.   [3] Mainly for drying.

Pears

State	Condition July 1			Production [1]		
	Average, 1929-38	1939	1940	Average, 1929-38	1939	Indicated July 1, 1940
	Percent	Percent	Percent	1,000 bu.	1,000 bu.	1,000 bu.
Maine	58	57	72	12	13	14
New Hampshire	64	58	63	14	11	13
Vermont	65	58	60	8	7	7
Massachusetts	60	57	55	72	53	50
Rhode Island	65	75	83	10	8	10
Connecticut	65	58	62	48	43	43
New York	47	55	60	1,374	1,749	1,855
New Jersey	54	60	69	73	52	53
Pennsylvania	50	62	64	630	918	886
Ohio	43	61	54	625	956	816
Indiana	43	60	55	350	527	476
Illinois	42	57	51	545	668	554
Michigan	52	54	55	1,042	1,354	1,419
Iowa	46	71	71	99	189	146
Missouri	36	50	46	347	426	420
Nebraska	42	62	62	41	55	46
Kansas	37	51	62	157	151	212
Delaware	52	56	77	15	9	11
Maryland	49	47	70	94	81	104
Virginia	36	21	45	325	189	392
West Virginia	27	32	53	56	56	92
North Carolina	46	39	46	260	230	253
South Carolina	53	63	66	100	104	112
Georgia	51	47	65	272	281	381
Florida	60	43	81	100	69	168
Kentucky	32	28	43	195	206	280
Tennessee	34	32	14	226	244	114
Alabama	47	50	40	280	312	248
Mississippi	49	51	52	278	348	372
Arkansas	44	56	46	152	211	177
Louisiana	52	47	81	115	130	204
Oklahoma	30	37	27	113	92	68
Texas	43	57	68	359	406	511
Idaho	64	62	79	60	62	67
Colorado	62	45	86	273	173	255
New Mexico	45	52	60	42	45	52
Arizona	60	85	54	12	11	8
Utah	64	65	78	86	104	118
Nevada	65	70	60	4	3	3
Washington, all	70	69	76	4,781	5,779	6,899
Bartlett		68	76	3,480	3,700	4,131
Other		71	76	1,301	2,079	2,268
Oregon, all	70	80	77	3,159	4,229	4,332
Bartlett		79	78	1,364	1,620	1,618
Other		81	76	1,814	2,609	2,714
California, all	66	68	68	9,530	10,542	9,459
Bartlett		69	67	8,417	9,209	8,042
Other		64	74	1,113	1,333	1,417
United States	59	63	65	26,333	31,047	31,240

[1] For some States in certain years, production includes some quantities unharvested on account of market conditions.

Cherries

State	All varieties						Sweet varieties		Sour varieties	
	Condition July 1			Production [1]			Production [1]		Production [1]	
	Average, 1929-38	1939	1940	Average, 1929-38	1939	Indicated July 1, 1940	1939	Indicated July 1, 1940	1939	Indicated July 1, 1940
	Percent	Percent	Percent	Tons	Tons	Tons	Tons	Tons	Tons	Tons
New York	60	75	61	19,094	27,980	23,100	1,980	1,650	25,970	21,450
Pennsylvania	51	70	70	7,491	12,170	11,760	3,980	3,450	8,890	8,310
Ohio	50	80	63	4,696	8,860	7,150	450	360	8,410	6,800
Michigan	54	64	65	28,310	37,000	39,010	2,730	3,730	34,270	35,280
Wisconsin	66	63	82	8,534	8,500	11,300			8,500	11,390
Montana	71	83	82	503	300	350	60	70	300	280
Idaho	68	65	80	2,698	1,900	2,060	1,370	1,580	430	480
Colorado	49	43	48	3,559	3,920	3,690	180	270	3,770	3,420
Utah	63	54	76	2,922	2,450	5,170	1,380	3,400	1,070	1,770
Washington	58	71	80	16,850	25,800	30,500	20,000	22,400	6,800	8,100
Oregon	56	76	74	13,990	21,200	22,000	18,500	19,300	2,700	2,700
California	[2] 60	[2] 82	[2] 32	20,720	36,000	14,100	36,000	14,100		
12 States	58	72	68	129,367	187,010	170,290	85,900	70,310	101,110	99,980

[1] For some States in certain years, production includes some quantities unharvested on account of market conditions.
[2] Production in percentage of a full crop.

Estimated Crop Conditions July 1, 1940, With Comparisons—Continued

Grapes

State	Condition July 1			Production [1]		
	Average, 1929–38	1939	1940	Average, 1929–38	1939	Indicated July 1, 1940
	Percent	Percent	Percent	Tons	Tons	Tons
Maine	74	71	74	31	30	30
New Hampshire	76	84	70	90	110	100
Vermont	72	85	95	39	50	50
Massachusetts	78	72	79	644	700	730
Rhode Island	82	80	89	288	230	310
Connecticut	80	75	80	2,083	2,460	2,640
New York	72	78	73	74,910	73,600	68,700
New Jersey	80	70	81	3,180	3,100	3,700
Pennsylvania	70	80	75	21,770	28,200	22,400
Ohio	67	85	80	27,430	42,800	40,400
Indiana	70	84	75	4,080	4,800	4,400
Illinois	73	85	75	6,490	5,800	7,800
Michigan	69	82	81	57,960	58,100	58,400
Wisconsin	75	83	84	387	490	490
Minnesota	70	82	70	257	290	270
Iowa	75	85	84	5,630	5,800	5,700
Missouri	72	85	71	9,380	12,500	10,300
Nebraska	64	67	77	2,520	3,000	3,900
Kansas	68	81	76	3,650	4,100	4,300
Delaware	85	88	82	2,050	2,000	1,900
Maryland	75	82	80	686	750	700
Virginia	76	74	73	2,280	2,600	2,700
West Virginia	62	76	75	1,298	1,750	1,850
North Carolina	78	77	77	6,224	7,500	8,000
South Carolina	72	75	71	1,465	2,020	1,960
Georgia	71	74	71	1,411	1,830	1,890
Florida	69	69	77	785	670	860
Kentucky	72	81	71	1,855	2,750	2,660
Tennessee	71	77	54	1,885	2,240	1,850
Alabama	71	74	57	1,275	1,710	1,430
Mississippi	69	71	54	285	290	220
Arkansas	73	69	56	9,840	8,200	8,600
Louisiana	61	60	67	54	50	60
Oklahoma	65	62	63	3,165	3,200	3,400
Texas	64	70	67	2,410	2,800	2,800
Idaho	82	83	89	539	580	580
Colorado	68	71	91	512	500	710
New Mexico	77	79	86	1,069	1,170	1,220
Arizona	81	75	92	1,047	710	760
Utah	83	80	89	952	840	910
Nevada	82	75	91	94	110	100
Washington	84	92	87	5,030	5,700	6,000
Oregon	85	88	88	2,280	1,700	2,200
California, all	79	85	78	1,950,700	2,228,000	2,134,000
Wine varieties	80	83	82	481,800	569,000	570,000
Raisin varieties	78	87	76	1,126,500	1,266,000	1,182,000
Dried [2]				212,560	245,000	
Not dried				276,200	289,000	
Table varieties	78	83	79	342,400	390,000	382,000
United States	78	85	78	2,220,001	2,525,830	2,421,930

[1] For some States in certain years, production includes some quantities unharvested on account of market conditions.
[2] Dried basis: 1 ton of dried raisins equivalent to 4 tons of fresh grapes.

Miscellaneous Fruits and Nuts in California, Oregon, Washington, and Florida

State and crop	Condition July 1			Production [1]		
	Average, 1929–38	1939	1940	Average, 1929–38	1939	Indicated July 1, 1940
	Pct.	Pct.	Pct.	Tons	Tons	Tons
California:						
Apricots	60	81	25	231,000	312,000	102,000
Figs:						
Dried	} 78	75	87	{ 22,260	26,000	
Not dried				8,690	9,800	
Olives	60	44	74	24,120	22,000	
Almonds	56	75	43	13,270	19,200	11,800
Walnuts	75	83	69	42,030	55,000	47,000
Oregon:						
Filberts	[2] 72	88	69	1,025	3,100	
Walnuts	[2] 71	78	75	2,340	4,400	
Washington:						
Apricots		80	85	6,710	10,700	12,600
Filberts		80	80	[3] 199	590	
Florida:						
Avocados	68	59	30	1,338 Boxes	2,500 Boxes	
Pineapples	75	67	55	14,250	15,000	

[1] For some States in certain years, production includes some quantities unharvested on account of market conditions. In 1939, estimates of such quantities were as follows (tons): California apricots, 8,000.
[3] Short-time average.

Plums and Prunes

Crop and State	Condition July 1			Production		
	Average, 1929–38	1939	1940	Average, 1929–38	1939	Indicated July 1, 1940
	Pct.	Pct.	Pct.	FRESH BASIS		
				Tons	Tons	Tons
Plums:						
Michigan	52	56	66	5,390	6,300	6,200
California	69	77	74	61,500	71,000	72,000
Prunes:						
Idaho	65	80	80	17,960	23,500	18,800
Washington, all	58	85	84	33,050	34,300	19,000
Eastern Washington	69	80	82	13,250	14,300	14,600
Western Washington	52	88	25	19,800	20,000	4,400
Oregon, all	54	88	28	113,650	153,800	37,900
Eastern Oregon	67	73	79	12,880	13,800	14,900
Western Oregon	53	90	22	100,770	140,000	33,000
California	64	62	65	198,900 [2]	185,000	202,000

[1] For some States in certain years, production includes some quantities unharvested on account of market conditions. In 1939, estimates of such quantities were as follows (tons): Plums, California, 7,000; Prunes: Idaho, 1,800; Eastern Washington, 500; Western Washington, 4,800; Eastern Oregon, 1,200; Western Oregon, 18,300.
[2] In California, the drying ratio is approximately 2½ pounds of fresh fruit to 1 pound dried.

Disposition of Prunes in Washington and Oregon [1]

State and disposition	Average, 1929–38	1939
	Tons	Tons
	FRESH BASIS	
Used fresh:		
Washington	14,210	15,800
Oregon	16,960	20,100
Canned: [2]		
Washington	4,540	6,800
Oregon	14,450	25,700
	DRY BASIS [3]	
Dried:		
Washington	3,450	1,800
Oregon	24,090	26,600

[1] An estimate of the disposition of the 1940 crop in Washington and Oregon will be published in October.
[2] Includes small quantities for cold packing.
[3] The drying ratio in Washington and Oregon ranges from 3 to 4 pounds of fresh fruit to 1 pound dried.

Citrus Fruits

Crop and State	Production [1]				Condition July 1 [1]		
	Average, 1928–37	1937	1938	1939	Average, 1929–38	1939	1940
	1,000 boxes	1,000 boxes	1,000 boxes	1,000 boxes	Per-cent	Per-cent	Per-cent
Oranges:							
California, all	34,715	45,914	41,152	44,820	76	67	75
Valencias	19,380	29,234	23,245	27,200	77	70	72
Navels and miscellaneous	15,335	16,680	17,907	17,620	74	64	79
Florida, all	17,842	26,700	33,900	27,800	71	76	62
Early and midseason	[3] 11,120	13,700	17,500	15,600			62
Valencias	[3] 7,180	10,700	13,000	9,900			62
Tangerines	[3] 2,260	2,300	3,400	2,300	83	52	66
Satsumas					54	57	42
Texas	677	1,440	2,815	2,360	65	69	63
Arizona	180	350	430	520	78	67	73
Alabama	78	74	96	75			75
Mississippi	39	67	85	50			53 [3]
Louisiana	255	238	385	360	[4] 85	73	54
7 States [4]	53,785	74,785	78,863	75,862	74	71	69
Grapefruit:							
Florida, all	12,838	14,600	23,600	15,800	65	53	62
Seedless	[3] 4,480	5,500	7,900	6,800			62
Other	[3] 9,540	9,100	15,700	9,000			62
Texas	3,538	11,800	15,670	13,900	60	65	53
Arizona	1,003	2,750	2,700	2,900	81	63	72
California	1,544	1,943	1,744	1,975	78	70	73
4 States [4]	18,923	31,093	43,714	34,575	66	59	60
Lemons: California [4]	7,881	9,360	11,322	12,000	74	66	78
Limes: Florida	20	70	95	95	73	74	37

[1] Relates to crop from bloom of year shown. In California the picking season adopted extends from Nov. 1 to Oct. 31. In other States the season begins about Sept. 1. For some States, in certain years, production includes some quantities donated to charity and/or eliminated on account of market conditions. Indicated production for the 1940-41 season will be issued in October.
[2] Short-time average.
[3] Failure reported.
[4] Net content of boxes varies. In California and Arizona the approximate average for oranges is 70 pounds net and grapefruit 60 pounds; in Florida and other States oranges 90 pounds and grapefruit 80 pounds; California lemons, about 76 pounds net.

Index Numbers of Prices Received and Paid by Farmers

Year and month	Index numbers of prices received (August 1909–July 1914=100)										Prices paid by farmers for commodities used in (1910–14=100)[1]	Ratio of prices received to prices paid
	Grains	Cotton and cottonseed	Fruits	Truck crops	Meat animals	Dairy products	Chickens and eggs	All groups	Living	Production	Living and production	
1938	74	70	73	101	114	109	108	95	122	124	122	78
1939	72	73	77	105	110	104	94	93	120	122	121	77
1939:												
January	66	71	76	98	112	109	97	94			120	78
February	66	70	78	105	116	107	91	92			120	77
March	66	71	81	110	116	100	88	91	119	122	120	76
April	67	70	82	95	114	95	87	89			120	74
May	72	72	85	88	112	92	85	90			120	75
June	73	73	93	105	107	94	83	89	119	121	120	74
1940:												
January	90	85	66	117	103	119	91	99			122	81
February	91	85	76	106	101	118	98	101			122	83
March	92	85	73	128	102	114	83	97	121	125	123	79
April	96	85	81	145	104	110	82	98			123	[2]80
May	92	83	88	133	108	104	84	98			[2]123	[2]80
June	83	81	104	134	102	104	81	95			[2]123	[2]77

[1] These index numbers are based on retail prices paid by farmers for commodities used in living and production reported quarterly for March, June, September, and December. The indexes for other months are interpolations between the successive quarterly indexes.

[2] Preliminary.

Pounds of Milk Produced per Milk Cow in Herds Kept by Reporters on July 1, 1940, With Comparisons, Averages for Grand Divisions, and Details for Some of the Included States

[State averages calculated by dividing the reported total daily milk production on the 1st of each July by the number of milk cows in milk or dry on the farms reporting. Figures for New England States are based on combined returns from crop and special dairy reporters and are weighted by counties. Figures for other States, regions, and United States are based on returns from crop reporters only. The United States average is based on about 20,000 herds. To reduce to quarts divide by 2.15]

State	10-year average, 1929–38	1938	1939	1940
Maine	16.4	17.1	17.5	17.3
New Hampshire	17.0	17.2	17.4	17.7
Vermont	17.5	17.1	18.4	19.6
Massachusetts	18.8	19.2	18.8	19.5
Connecticut	18.5	19.7	20.5	19.2
New York	20.3	21.7	21.4	22.9
New Jersey	20.2	20.1	20.0	20.9
Pennsylvania	19.5	19.8	19.5	21.3
North Atlantic	19.64	20.16	20.14	21.31
Ohio	18.6	19.4	18.9	20.0
Indiana	16.7	17.6	17.5	18.1
Illinois	16.8	18.2	18.3	18.5
Michigan	21.1	21.4	21.5	22.2
Wisconsin	21.4	22.2	22.5	22.7
East North Central	19.48	20.34	20.41	20.72
Minnesota	19.4	21.2	20.3	20.7
Iowa	17.3	18.3	17.9	18.3
Missouri	12.0	12.8	13.1	13.6
North Dakota	17.6	19.2	19.7	19.4
South Dakota	15.8	16.5	16.9	17.2
Nebraska	16.1	16.2	18.1	17.6
Kansas	15.0	15.7	15.7	15.2
West North Central	16.40	17.56	17.56	17.59
Maryland	15.9	16.8	17.0	17.5
Virginia	13.6	14.0	13.2	13.8
West Virginia	14.7	15.1	14.8	14.7
North Carolina	12.7	13.6	13.8	13.3
South Carolina	9.3	11.3	10.9	12.7
Georgia	9.3	9.7	10.1	10.0
South Atlantic	12.25	13.38	12.80	13.17
Kentucky	13.6	13.4	14.1	14.6
Tennessee	11.6	13.1	12.8	13.1
Mississippi	8.4	8.5	9.0	8.1
Arkansas	10.2	10.6	10.7	10.4
Oklahoma	12.2	13.5	14.1	13.0
Texas	10.3	11.7	10.7	10.5
South Central	10.67	11.22	11.54	11.04
Montana	17.3	20.2	21.2	19.3
Idaho	21.0	21.5	21.9	21.8
Wyoming	16.1	16.4	17.8	19.8
Colorado	16.5	18.0	17.4	18.7
Washington	21.3	23.4	22.2	22.8
Oregon	19.5	20.4	20.3	20.7
California	19.4	21.0	20.9	20.4
Western	18.18	19.20	20.17	20.16
United States	16.30	17.19	17.27	17.43

Farm Employment: Index Numbers, 1940, With Comparisons

[Annual average 1910–14=100]

Date	Unadjusted			Adjusted for seasonal variation		
	Total employment	Family workers	Hired workers	Total employment	Family workers	Hired workers
1935	93	95	85	93	95	85
1936	91	93	86	91	93	86
1937	90	90	88	90	90	88
1938	89	90	87	89	90	87
1939	88	89	86	88	89	86
1940:						
January 1	72	77	55	89	92	79
February 1	73	77	59	87	89	82
March 1	75	79	64	85	88	80
April 1	81	84	73	84	86	78
May 1	91	92	87	85	85	81
June 1	99	100	96	85	87	81
July 1	100	97	108	88	87	89

Farm Labor Supply and Demand, July 1, 1939 and 1940

State and division	Farm labor supply, percentage of normal		Farm labor demand, percentage of normal		Supply expressed as percentage of demand	
	1939	1940	1939	1940	1939	1940
Maine	90	87	86	90	105	97
New Hampshire	77	81	96	87	80	93
Vermont	86	85	97	94	89	90
Massachusetts	91	81	88	84	103	96
Rhode Island	99	95	99	95	100	100
Connecticut	84	85	88	94	95	90
New England	87.5	84.3	89.9	89.5	97.3	94.2
New York	86	83	84	90	102	92
New Jersey	92	84	87	90	106	94
Pennsylvania	87	84	86	90	101	93
Middle Atlantic	87.3	83.6	85.3	89.9	102.3	93.0
Ohio	87	85	85	88	102	97
Indiana	92	88	88	91	105	97
Illinois	91	89	88	90	103	99
Michigan	90	85	89	91	101	93
Wisconsin	95	91	87	93	109	98
East North Central	90.9	87.8	87.3	90.6	104.1	96.9
Minnesota	95	94	85	87	112	108
Iowa	95	90	89	91	107	104
Missouri	84	84	87	86	97	98
North Dakota	91	93	69	76	132	132
South Dakota	90	89	68	75	132	119
Nebraska	93	94	73	73	127	129
Kansas	94	94	76	86	124	109
West North Central	91.8	91.7	81.9	84.9	112.1	108.0
Delaware	94	90	87	96	108	94
Maryland	90	84	94	96	96	88
Virginia	89	84	88	92	101	91
West Virginia	87	87	83	87	105	100
North Carolina	87	88	90	87	97	101
South Carolina	80	79	84	85	95	93
Georgia	79	81	89	88	89	92
Florida	86	89	84	78	102	114
South Atlantic	84.4	83.8	87.9	87.8	96.0	95.4
Kentucky	87	89	89	88	98	101
Tennessee	85	90	90	85	94	106
Alabama	81	86	91	84	89	102
Mississippi	80	87	89	84	90	104
East South Central	83.0	87.9	89.7	85.1	92.5	103.4
Arkansas	83	85	84	78	99	109
Louisiana	86	86	85	86	101	100
Oklahoma	91	92	78	81	117	114
Texas	92	91	74	82	124	111
West South Central	89.4	89.4	78.2	81.9	114.3	109.1
Montana	97	95	81	89	120	107
Idaho	103	95	86	95	120	100
Wyoming	98	94	83	81	116	106
Colorado	96	94	79	82	122	115
New Mexico	93	91	75	77	124	118
Arizona	97	95	79	83	123	114
Utah	97	95	78	79	125	114
Nevada	97	97	87	80	120	108
Mountain	97.2	93.9	80.3	85.5	121.0	109.9
Washington	102	97	83	94	123	93
Oregon	100	90	89	93	112	97
California	101	97	85	87	119	111
Pacific	101.0	92.9	85.4	90.1	118.3	103.1
United States	89.6	88.4	84.6	86.7	105.9	102.0

Average Prices Received by Farmers for Farm Products, June 15, 1939 and 1940 by States

State and division	Wheat, per bushel		Corn, per bushel		Oats, per bushel		Barley, per bushel		Rye, per bushel		Buckwheat, per bushel		Flaxseed, per bushel		Grain sorghums, per 100 pounds		Soybeans, per bushel		Potatoes, per bushel		Sweetpotatoes, per bushel		Hay (all loose), per ton		Cotton (lint), per pound		Cottonseed, per ton		Apples, per bushel	
	1939	1940	1939	1940	1939	1940	1939	1940	1939	1940	1939	1940	1939	1940	1939	1940	1939	1940	1939	1940	1939	1940	1939	1940	1939	1940	1939	1940	1939	1940
	Ct.	Ct.	Ct.	Ct.	Ct.	Ct.	Ct.	Ct.	Ct.	Ct.	Ct.	Ct.	Dol.	Dol.	Dol.	Dol.	Dol.	Dol.	Ct.	Ct.	Ct.	Ct.	Dol.	Dol.	Ct.	Ct.	Dol.	Dol.	Dol.	Dol.
Maine	120	125	72	75	49	45	70	80	----	----	85	85	----	----	----	----	----	----	40	90	----	----	7.90	8.40	----	----	----	----	1.30	1.20
New Hampshire	----	----	75	75	52	60	----	----	----	----	----	----	----	----	----	----	----	----	90	135	----	----	9.80	13.00	----	----	----	----	1.55	1.20
Vermont	----	----	75	75	52	64	70	80	----	----	80	80	----	----	----	----	----	----	100	120	----	----	8.90	10.10	----	----	----	----	1.40	1.15
Massachusetts	----	----	75	75	52	62	----	----	----	----	----	----	----	----	----	----	----	----	95	130	----	----	15.70	16.80	----	----	----	----	1.30	1.30
Rhode Island	----	----	75	75	52	62	----	----	----	----	----	----	----	----	----	----	----	----	95	120	----	----	15.00	16.50	----	----	----	----	1.30	1.20
Connecticut	----	----	75	75	52	62	----	----	----	----	----	----	----	----	----	----	----	----	90	120	----	----	14.50	17.00	----	----	----	----	1.30	1.20
New England	----	----	----	----	50.0	50.4	70.0	80.0	----	----	84.1	83.5	----	----	----	----	----	----	49.1	97.2	----	----	10.66	11.98	----	----	----	----	1.33	1.23
New York	79	85	63	72	41	46	52	55	58	60	54	70	----	----	----	----	1.00	1.25	75	85	----	----	7.40	13.20	----	----	----	----	1.00	1.00
New Jersey	86	98	65	76	40	49	58	66	60	67	66	75	----	----	----	----	----	1.20	90	115	145	150	14.20	17.90	----	----	----	----	1.25	1.40
Pennsylvania	80	90	62	73	39	47	52	59	60	69	54	67	----	----	----	----	1.15	1.20	90	100	----	----	8.80	13.40	----	----	----	----	1.15	.95
Middle Atlantic	80.0	89.2	62.4	73.2	39.9	46.5	52.1	57.2	59.6	66.9	54.1	68.6	----	----	----	----	----	1.20	83.2	94.9	----	----	8.20	13.47	----	----	----	----	1.08	1.04
Ohio	68	78	51	62	33	36	44	44	48	50	55	59	----	----	----	----	.80	.73	75	95	----	----	5.60	6.40	----	----	----	----	1.20	.85
Indiana	67	75	47	62	30	33	45	48	42	45	49	50	----	----	----	----	.80	.76	75	105	110	125	5.40	7.30	----	----	----	----	1.15	1.30
Illinois	66	74	44	59	29	30	41	44	41	43	50	50	----	----	----	----	.80	.73	90	110	80	105	5.70	6.20	----	----	----	----	1.35	1.50
Michigan	64	75	50	61	34	34	51	47	41	37	48	50	1.55	1.60	----	----	.85	.70	45	85	----	----	6.20	7.50	----	----	----	----	1.50	.90
Wisconsin	70	74	50	61	32	34	54	50	44	44	53	51	1.60	1.57	----	----	.90	.75	50	65	----	----	7.00	7.70	----	----	----	----	1.15	1.25
East North Central	66.6	75.6	46.7	60.5	31.1	32.7	51.5	48.5	42.9	43.7	51.0	52.4	1.57	1.58	----	----	.80	.74	56.2	84.3	90.0	112.5	6.15	7.06	----	----	----	----	1.35	1.06
Minnesota	66	67	38	49	26	27	36	37	38	32	50	49	1.62	1.55	----	----	----	.85	49	55	----	----	3.50	3.80	----	----	----	----	1.30	1.15
Iowa	63	73	40	56	27	30	36	40	37	39	63	60	1.60	1.50	----	----	.80	.81	85	100	85	130	5.20	6.20	----	----	----	----	1.40	1.45
Missouri	64	75	49	65	30	38	44	47	51	46	70	73	1.55	1.65	1.40	1.40	1.05	1.25	[1]80	110	85	110	5.30	5.80	8.7	10.0	22.00	24.00	1.50	1.65
North Dakota	60	57	42	43	23	22	32	29	33	25	60	60	1.55	1.51	----	----	----	----	55	55	----	----	3.50	3.30	----	----	----	----	----	----
South Dakota	62	60	39	50	25	26	33	36	35	29	50	45	1.59	1.49	.95	.85	----	----	75	65	----	----	4.00	3.90	----	----	----	----	1.40	----
Nebraska	62	70	45	62	26	38	32	48	36	46	----	----	1.60	1.55	.85	1.00	----	----	80	90	----	----	4.00	5.80	----	----	----	----	1.50	1.20
Kansas	01	65	50	67	30	38	36	46	40	45	----	----	1.60	1.60	.90	1.25	1.20	1.25	75	100	85	120	4.00	4.80	----	----	----	----	1.35	1.10
West North Central	61.8	64.4	41.9	56.4	26.7	29.5	34.3	37.2	35.5	32.3	53.2	51.9	1.60	1.54	.96	1.15	.83	.85	[1]68.4	71.4	85.0	115.0	4.21	4.90	----	----	----	----	1.41	1.41
Delaware	81	92	62	71	45	48	----	----	70	64	60	68	----	----	----	----	.80	.95	95	115	105	90	11.80	15.00	----	----	----	----	1.15	1.2
Maryland	82	89	61	72	45	47	49	54	68	64	59	66	----	----	----	----	.85	1.05	85	110	110	110	9.80	12.80	----	----	----	----	1.15	.10
Virginia	84	97	70	77	44	53	55	61	74	78	73	81	----	----	----	----	1.05	1.05	[1]81	85	100	90	11.00	12.40	9.0	10.0	24.00	24.00	1.05	1.10
West Virginia	85	96	73	81	44	49	52	59	70	69	72	82	----	----	----	----	1.30	1.40	95	100	----	----	9.60	10.20	----	----	----	----	1.20	.90
North Carolina	90	101	73	74	46	53	65	75	87	97	74	78	----	----	----	----	.95	1.05	65	80	65	80	12.80	13.90	9.2	9.9	24.10	28.80	1.20	1.05
South Carolina	81	95	58	83	36	50	----	----	110	104	----	----	----	----	----	----	1.60	2.20	70	80	75	75	12.80	13.20	9.3	10.3	24.20	27.20	1.00	----
Georgia	86	96	62	98	40	53	----	----	102	98	----	----	----	----	----	----	2.45	2.30	60	90	75	80	11.80	13.50	9.2	10.3	24.00	27.70	1.25	1.20
Florida	----	----	71	95	50	70	----	----	----	----	----	----	----	----	----	----	----	----	60	100	80	90	11.50	12.00	9.2	9.9	20.60	21.60	----	----
South Atlantic	84.3	95.0	66.2	81.5	40.4	51.5	53.0	58.3	80.9	82.8	69.7	78.4	----	----	----	----	1.01	1.11	[1]74.1	89.1	76.9	82.1	11.27	12.73	9.2	10.2	24.11	27.72	1.12	1.07
Kentucky	72	87	61	78	38	47	54	60	61	88	72	75	----	----	----	----	1.05	1.45	90	110	80	100	7.90	10.40	----	----	----	----	1.00	.90
Tennessee	83	98	67	85	44	53	60	68	80	88	73	85	----	----	----	----	1.20	1.65	[1]60	110	70	100	9.00	12.20	8.4	8.9	22.50	26.40	1.10	1.00
Alabama	84	102	67	99	46	59	----	----	----	----	----	----	----	----	----	----	2.40	2.90	[1]55	60	75	90	9.20	11.40	8.9	9.3	23.00	26.20	1.05	----
Mississippi	----	----	67	86	39	44	----	----	----	----	----	----	----	----	----	----	1.55	1.80	[1]47	75	80	90	8.50	9.50	8.6	9.7	22.40	24.90	1.05	----
East South Central	76.4	92.6	65.2	85.1	42.8	51.1	56.8	63.8	72.4	88.0	72.5	80.0	----	----	----	----	1.44	1.81	[1]67.3	87.6	75.9	92.8	8.58	10.91	8.7	9.5	22.48	25.44	1.05	.94
Arkansas	71	81	63	78	38	43	----	----	----	----	----	----	----	----	1.10	1.60	1.15	1.50	[1]60	70	80	100	7.50	7.80	8.3	9.3	21.90	23.40	1.15	1.25
Louisiana	----	----	64	74	39	43	----	----	----	----	----	----	----	----	----	----	1.15	1.55	60	80	80	85	8.30	9.50	8.4	9.3	23.00	24.40	1.45	----
Oklahoma	59	62	56	70	31	31	33	39	41	46	----	----	----	----	.97	1.25	1.50	1.80	55	75	95	120	4.70	6.50	8.0	8.4	21.20	24.70	1.30	1.25
Texas	62	63	56	68	28	27	37	38	49	49	----	----	----	1.60	.88	1.15	1.65	1.90	70	80	95	100	7.60	7.60	8.3	9.0	22.60	24.60	1.15	----
West South Central	60.2	62.4	58.7	71.4	29.8	30.0	34.7	38.7	----	46.3	----	----	----	----	.90	1.17	1.24	1.51	[1]61.6	75.9	85.5	94.0	6.74	7.52	8.3	9.1	22.25	24.06	1.19	1.25
Montana	53	54	58	62	28	30	37	38	29	30	----	----	1.50	1.40	----	----	----	----	90	120	----	----	4.70	4.50	----	----	----	----	.70	1.20
Idaho	49	59	54	70	30	29	37	48	45	60	----	----	----	1.65	----	----	----	----	28	80	----	----	6.00	6.90	----	----	----	----	.85	.65
Wyoming	54	72	60	68	33	38	46	53	34	51	----	----	----	----	----	----	----	----	90	80	----	----	6.50	7.70	----	----	----	----	1.55	----
Colorado	55	66	55	71	33	42	36	56	34	53	----	----	----	----	.75	1.10	----	----	70	85	----	----	6.50	7.30	----	----	----	----	.80	1.05
New Mexico	58	71	68	77	36	42	46	56	----	----	----	----	----	----	.85	1.20	----	----	85	105	----	----	8.00	10.00	7.9	9.8	22.00	27.00	1.20	----
Arizona	75	80	81	95	42	50	48	53	----	----	----	----	----	1.85	1.00	1.20	----	----	50	105	----	----	7.60	7.50	10.1	10.7	22.00	23.00	1.25	1.20
Utah	52	69	74	87	35	43	41	57	48	60	----	----	----	----	----	----	----	----	50	80	----	----	7.60	8.00	----	----	----	----	1.00	1.60
Nevada	72	77	72	90	50	47	59	50	----	----	----	----	----	----	----	----	----	----	60	85	----	----	8.00	7.00	----	----	----	----	1.55	----
Mountain	52.8	58.6	57.5	70.9	30.7	33.8	38.2	50.0	32.4	48.0	----	----	----	1.49	.82	1.19	----	----	44.3	83.0	----	----	6.24	6.69	9.4	10.4	22.00	23.80	.87	.88
Washington	58	60	60	72	42	34	50	45	60	65	----	----	----	1.70	----	----	----	----	65	85	----	----	7.60	7.30	----	----	----	----	.80	1.35
Oregon	61	65	65	73	43	32	55	50	55	63	----	----	----	1.65	----	----	----	----	60	90	----	----	8.20	6.80	----	----	----	----	.80	.90
California	72	78	72	83	42	29	44	33	58	62	----	----	1.73	1.75	1.15	1.25	----	----	[1]45	80	100	175	8.20	6.20	9.0	9.5	24.00	29.00	.50	.70
Pacific	60.8	63.8	68.5	78.0	42.4	32.4	45.5	36.2	56.0	63.5	----	----	----	1.74	----	----	----	----	[1]52.8	82.9	----	----	8.07	6.59	----	----	----	----	.75	1.20
United States	62.5	67.4	49.9	63.5	29.9	32.7	39.4	40.8	39.1	40.3	55.9	67.2	1.61	1.56	.92	1.17	.83	.79	[1]61.0	85.7	80.5	92.2	6.63	7.71	8.67	9.54	22.72	25.54	1.02	1.11

Average Prices Received by Farmers for Farm Products, June 15, 1940, With Comparisons

Date	Wheat, per bushel	Corn, per bushel	Oats, per bushel	Barley, per bushel	Rye, per bushel	Buckwheat, per bushel	Potatoes, per bushel	Sweetpotatoes, per bushel	Flaxseed, per bushel	Apples, per bushel	Cotton, per pound	Cottonseed, per ton	Butterfat, per pound	Milk (whole) wholesale, 100 lb.	Eggs, per dozen	Chickens, per pound
	Cents	Cents	Cents	Cents	Cents	Cents	Cents	Cents	Dollars	Dollars	Cents	Dollars	Cents	Dollars	Cents	Cents
5-year average, August 1909 to July 1914	88.4	64.2	39.9	61.9	72.0	73.0	69.7	87.8	1.69	0.96	12.40	22.55	26.3	1.60	21.5	11.4
June average, 1910–14	89.0	68.4	41.8	63.0	72.9	77.3	71.8	93.0	1.72	1.18	12.70	22.47	23.4	1.26	16.7	11.9
1936, June 15	79.9	61.3	24.3	37.0	43.8	57.2	136.6	87.4	1.47	1.07	11.38	27.31	27.7	1.64	18.9	16.4
1937, June 15	108.9	117.2	48.1	71.4	85.3	100.3	[1]88.4	105.8	1.73	1.56	12.47	35.62	30.8	1.75	17.6	14.8
1938, June 15	69.7	52.3	25.3	42.9	46.0	72.2	61.2	84.0	1.62	.77	8.12	21.29	23.7	1.52	18.2	15.7
1939, June 15	62.5	49.9	29.9	39.4	39.1	55.9	61.0	80.5	1.61	1.02	8.67	22.72	22.2	[1]1.43	14.9	13.4
July 15	55.7	47.8	26.5	35.5	34.3	56.4	76.4	83.5	1.39	.90	8.77	20.70	22.0	1.52	16.5	13.7
Aug. 15	54.5	45.7	25.4	34.5	34.2	54.8	69.1	90.7	1.35	.66	8.70	16.24	22.4	1.64	17.5	13.0
Sept. 15	72.7	56.2	31.5	42.8	44.0	59.7	69.4	77.5	1.53	.63	9.13	20.56	24.7	1.78	20.6	13.6
Oct. 15	70.3	47.6	30.3	42.2	45.1	62.7	66.4	68.0	1.63	.59	8.73	22.88	26.9	1.90	22.9	12.7
Nov. 15	73.1	46.8	32.1	42.2	44.6	62.4	69.2	64.5	1.64	.62	8.80	23.75	28.1	2.01	25.8	12.4
Dec. 15	82.4	50.3	34.7	43.8	52.3	61.7	70.8	68.6	1.80	.68	9.71	24.75	28.5	2.00	20.5	11.7
1940, Jan. 15	84.5	53.2	36.3	45.9	56.7	63.0	74.0	72.9	1.94	.73	10.09	26.00	30.0	1.97	18.3	12.0
Feb. 15	84.1	54.7	37.7	46.1	55.7	61.7	75.2	79.3	1.88	.81	9.97	26.64	29.7	1.94	20.2	12.2
Mar. 15	85.0	56.0	38.6	46.1	55.6	64.2	77.0	83.6	1.91	.85	9.96	26.84	28.4	1.84	15.4	12.8
Apr. 15	88.9	58.6	38.8	46.2	57.1	65.7	83.8	87.8	1.91	.90	10.03	27.18	27.5	1.75	15.0	12.9
May 15	80.7	63.4	36.6	45.3	52.4	66.7	83.5	91.2	1.75	1.01	9.79	26.69	26.9	[1]1.66	15.1	13.6
June 15	67.4	63.5	32.7	40.8	40.3	67.2	85.7	92.2	1.56	1.11	9.54	25.54	25.6	1.61	14.4	13.3

[1] Revised.

Average Prices Received by Farmers for Farm Products, June 15, 1939 and 1940, by States—Continued

State and division	Hogs, per 100 pounds		Beef cattle, per 100 pounds		Veal calves, per 100 pounds		Sheep, per 100 pounds		Lambs, per 100 pounds		Milk cows, per head		Horses, per head		Mules, per head		Chickens, per pound		Butter, per pound		Butterfat, per pound		Eggs, per dozen		Wool, per pound	
	1939	1940	1939	1940	1939	1940	1939	1940	1939	1940	1939	1940	1939	1940	1939	1940	1939	1940	1939	1940	1939	1940	1939	1940	1939	1940
	Dol.	Dol.	Dol.	Dol.	Dol.	Dol.	Dol.	Dol.	Dol.	Dol.	Dol.	Dol.	Dol.	Dol.	Dol.	Dol.	Ct.	Ct.	Ct.	Ct.	Ct.	Ct.	Ct.	Ct.	Ct	Ct
Maine	7.40	6.00	5.60	6.00	8.50	8.40	4.70	4.20	8.60	8.50	63	66	160	150	------	------	15.3	16.2	28	31	32	33	23.1	21.8	22	30
New Hampshire	6.70	5.80	5.40	5.90	8.40	8.40	4.10	4.00	8.50	8.70	78	82	145	130	------	------	15.4	16.2	27	30	30	32	23.6	22.9	23	28
Vermont	6.90	5.60	5.10	5.60	7.80	8.00	3.90	3.90	8.50	8.20	70	74	155	150	------	------	16.7	16.2	28	31	29	32	20.7	20.2	24	29
Massachusetts	6.70	5.60	5.40	5.90	7.80	8.00	4.00	4.00	8.80	9.00	93	98	155	150	------	------	16.8	16.6	28	31	30	33	24.9	23.3	24	27
Rhode Island	7.00	5.60	5.40	5.90	9.20	8.70	4.20	4.00	8.80	8.80	95	92	155	145	------	------	18.0	17.8	28	31	30	33	24.7	23.4	26	27
Connecticut	7.00	5.60	5.40	5.90	9.40	9.20	4.20	4.00	8.80	9.00	92	87	165	140	------	------	17.5	18.3	27	30	30	32	23.5	24.0	27	28
New Enlgand	6.91	5.60	5.37	5.84	8.27	8.31	.....	...	...	...	77.40	80.00	.....	150.00	....	.....	16.5	16.9	27.9	30.9	30.2	32.5	23.8	22.9	....	--
New York	6.80	5.40	5.60	5.90	8.60	9.10	3.85	3.90	8.80	9.00	70	80	153	142	157	150	16.9	16.8	26	29	22	26	20.0	19.0	23	29
New Jersey	7.20	5.60	6.50	6.10	10.40	10.30	5.00	5.20	10.50	10.30	115	115	145	130	156	135	19.3	19.0	28	29	29	30	23.	21.8	23	32
Pennsylvania	6.80	5.50	7.40	7.70	9.10	9.50	3.65	3.60	8.50	9.10	70	78	127	123	131	128	17.0	16.4	25	27	23	26	18.1	17.4	25	30
Middle Atlantic	6.83	5.47	6.71	7.01	8.89	9.32	3.75	3.75	8.65	9.05	72.60	81.40	138.80	131.80	------	------	17.4	17.0	25.5	27.9	22.5	26.0	19.7	18.7	24.0	29.5
Ohio	6.20	5.00	7.80	7.80	8.30	8.80	3.10	3.10	8.30	8.40	58	59	106	96	104	91	14.3	14.2	24	27	21	24	13.5	13.2	25	30
Indiana	6.10	4.95	7.70	7.70	8.30	8.80	2.90	2.90	8.50	9.20	60	64	101	90	111	97	13.0	13.4	25	29	21	25	12.6	12.2	25	31
Illinois	6.10	4.80	7.90	8.30	8.40	8.70	3.40	3.05	8.10	8.90	64	69	83	80	103	100	13.2	13.5	25	28	21	24	12.5	12.6	24	30
Michigan	6.00	5.00	6.90	7.20	8.60	9.20	3.00	3.20	8.40	9.10	62	67	123	105	110	110	14.4	13.5	25	27	23	27	14.3	13.5	25	33
Wisconsin	5.70	4.55	5.90	6.10	7.60	8.10	2.45	2.65	7.50	8.30	69	75	119	120	115	108	13.6	12.9	24	28	26	30	13.6	13.2	24	30
East North Central	6.07	4.87	7.53	7.75	8.11	8.59	3.05	3.05	8.25	8.73	64.00	68.50	101.70	94.80	105.60	97.90	13.6	13.6	24.6	27.6	23.0	26.6	13.8	13.0	24.8	30.8
Minnesota	5.90	4.65	6.80	6.80	8.00	8.50	3.15	3.00	8.30	8.60	60	64	94	84	91	92	10.7	10.3	24	28	24	28	12.6	12.1	23	29
Iowa	5.90	4.65	8.20	8.40	8.10	8.70	3.30	3.20	8.20	8.90	60	64	89	81	101	92	11.7	11.4	24	27	23	27	11.7	11.9	24	30
Missouri	6.00	4.70	7.90	7.70	8.30	8.50	3.70	3.50	8.30	9.00	50	51	77	70	102	97	11.6	10.9	24	26	20	22	11.4	11.0	24	31
North Dakota	5.50	4.20	6.30	6.50	7.50	7.60	3.20	3.10	7.40	7.50	55	59	71	65	78	70	10.0	9.4	23	26	21	24	11.1	10.9	20	26
South Dakota	5.70	4.60	7.40	7.60	7.90	8.20	3.00	3.25	7.60	8.10	56	58	68	62	77	74	10.7	10.0	23	27	24	24	11.2	10.9	22	28
Nebraska	5.70	4.70	7.80	7.80	8.10	8.70	3.60	4.20	8.40	9.10	58	60	69	64	84	81	11.5	10.5	23	27	20	22	11.2	10.8	18	24
Kansas	5.90	4.75	7.40	7.90	8.00	8.70	3.25	4.15	8.30	8.90	55	57	68	63	88	84	10.4	10.6	24	26	20	23	11.1	11.0	19	24
West North Central	5.88	4.66	7.64	7.78	8.03	8.49	3.31	3.42	8.08	8.62	57.10	60.00	77.80	71.20	94.90	90.60	11.2	10.8	23.7	26.5	22.1	25.6	11.6	11.4	22.1	28.1
Delaware	7.00	5.50	7.30	7.50	9.30	9.80	3.75	3.55	9.20	10.00	70	72	114	115	147	140	17.0	18.0	25	26	25	26	17.0	16.5	25	32
Maryland	6.90	5.30	7.70	7.20	8.90	9.30	3.40	3.40	9.60	10.20	69	75	119	112	137	130	16.8	18.4	23	24	23	25	17.4	16.2	26	32
Virginia	6.30	5.30	6.70	7.00	8.30	9.00	2.80	3.00	9.10	9.60	49	51	112	109	140	131	15.5	16.2	19	21	19	24	15.7	15.8	27	34
West Virginia	6.40	5.30	6.50	6.60	7.90	8.30	3.60	3.00	8.40	8.00	46	48	108	105	103	99	14.4	14.0	23	23	21	24	15.3	15.2	26	32
North Carolina	6.30	5.40	5.50	5.80	7.50	7.90	4.30	4.45	7.80	7.50	46	48	116	114	168	157	15.1	15.1	22	22	22	23	17.9	17.5	26	31
South Carolina	6.30	5.30	5.40	5.50	7.00	7.60	4.40	4.40	6.30	6.50	43	44	110	100	160	150	16.6	16.4	24	24	22	24	18.0	17.8	25	30
Georgia	5.90	5.20	5.40	5.80	7.00	7.60	4.10	3.80	6.10	6.40	41	42	105	100	154	145	15.6	15.4	22	23	20	22	16.5	17.0	23	24
Florida	5.70	5.00	5.10	5.40	6.30	6.30	3.20	3.50	6.00	6.10	44	47	98	87	135	120	18.2	17.5	28	28	29	28	20.0	19.4	22	26
South Atlantic	6.14	5.26	5.76	6.02	7.69	8.19	3.35	3.17	8.71	8.74	48.10	50.30	112.60	109.10	147.30	136.20	16.0	16.6	21.8	22.5	20.5	23.6	16.7	16.5	26.4	32.6
Kentucky	5.90	4.85	7.10	7.00	8.20	9.00	2.70	3.00	9.40	10.60	45	49	81	79	107	107	12.5	12.5	22	24	19	22	12.4	12.6	27	33
Tennessee	5.80	4.80	6.00	6.40	7.70	8.10	3.05	3.20	8.50	9.70	44	44	96	88	129	120	12.5	12.4	19	22	20	25	13.1	13.6	26	32
Alabama	5.70	4.80	5.20	5.30	6.80	7.20	3.90	3.40	7.00	7.60	39	40	87	85	132	125	13.7	13.1	21	22	21	23	14.6	15.0	21	24
Mississippi	5.40	4.50	5.00	5.20	6.50	7.00	3.30	3.40	4.90	5.60	34	37	77	77	118	118	14.4	14.0	24	25	21	24	14.5	14.9	20	25
East South Central	5.70	4.74	5.98	6.01	7.32	7.85	2.82	3.07	8.89	10.09	40.50	42.60	85.50	82.10	119.30	114.90	12.9	12.7	20.8	22.7	19.8	23.3	13.3	13.7	26.3	32.3
Arkansas	5.40	4.05	5.70	5.80	7.20	7.50	3.90	3.65	7.20	7.50	41	40	73	64	103	98	12.2	10.8	24	25	19	22	12.0	12.0	22	27
Louisiana	5.30	4.35	5.20	5.70	6.90	7.10	3.75	3.90	5.70	5.60	38	39	70	66	108	106	15.7	16.4	26	26	21	24	14.8	13.9	22	25
Oklahoma	5.60	4.70	6.10	6.60	7.50	8.10	3.40	4.30	8.00	8.70	44	46	63	55	88	78	11.2	10.2	25	27	20	22	11.6	11.4	17	22
Texas	5.80	4.90	6.20	6.60	7.80	8.10	4.35	4.85	5.90	7.10	41	44	56	49	88	79	11.6	11.5	25	26	19	22	11.9	11.3	21	29
West South Central	5.57	4.57	6.07	7.47	7.54	7.90	4.29	4.80	5.98	7.11	41.40	43.30	60.80	53.50	91.30	83.50	11.8	11.3	24.9	26.0	19.5	22.0	12.0	11.0	20.9	28.7
Montana	6.30	5.30	6.50	7.00	8.00	8.60	4.10	5.00	7.20	7.60	58	67	56	50	65	65	15.4	13.0	25	27	21	24	15.6	11.9	21	28
Idaho	6.40	5.20	6.10	6.50	7.30	8.10	4.20	3.70	7.30	8.00	59	62	70	65	76	70	12.4	11.0	26	29	23	26	16.1	13.2	21	31
Wyoming	6.20	4.85	6.90	7.10	8.30	8.40	4.40	4.15	7.70	8.20	61	59	76	64	87	85	14.0	13.6	25	28	22	24	14.7	13.1	21	27
Colorado	6.10	4.95	7.40	7.50	8.80	9.40	3.80	3.60	8.50	9.20	54	58	68	57	91	80	12.6	12.2	25	26	20	22	13.1	12.8	21	29
New Mexico	6.00	5.00	5.40	6.70	7.00	8.10	3.00	2.80	7.00	7.00	50	50	50	49	70	65	14.0	13.5	25	26	20	24	14.5	15.7	20	27
Arizona	6.90	5.60	7.00	7.00	7.60	8.70	2.50	3.00	8.00	8.30	58	65	70	70	85	87	19.8	16.5	27	29	24	28	22.0	22.0	20	26
Utah	6.60	5.30	6.30	6.70	7.90	9.00	3.40	3.50	7.40	8.00	55	60	72	65	80	75	12.8	10.9	28	30	25	28	17.4	16.0	19	26
Nevada	6.90	5.40	7.30	7.00	8.00	8.30	3.40	3.40	7.60	8.20	68	73	75	85	90	92	18.4	16.5	28	30	26	29	21.5	18.1	20	26
Mountain	6.30	5.08	6.59	6.99	7.98	8.68	3.80	3.83	7.57	8.03	55.60	60.70	65.10	58.90	84.30	73.90	13.6	12.3	25.6	27.6	21.9	24.7	16.0	14.4	20.5	27.7
Washington	6.90	5.80	6.80	6.70	7.90	8.40	3.40	3.55	7.50	7.80	59	65	76	62	86	71	14.0	13.6	26	29	23	27	18.1	17.3	20	25
Oregon	6.80	5.60	6.80	7.00	7.50	8.50	3.40	3.90	7.30	7.80	52	56	73	64	76	68	14.4	12.9	26	29	23	27	17.1	14.6	22	28
California	6.90	5.80	7.00	7.30	7.70	9.00	3.70	3.50	7.80	8.30	65	73	88	86	86	92	15.1	16.0	26	30	26	30	18.9	17.0	23	29
Pacific	6.88	5.76	6.91	7.12	7.71	8.73	3.57	3.63	7.61	8.09	60.70	67.40	78.30	70.90	82.70	78.80	14.7	15.0	26.0	29.3	24.3	28.2	18.5	16.8	22.4	28.2
United States	5.96	4.82	6.81	7.10	7.98	8.46	3.67	3.81	7.49	8.12	57.20	61.10	81.30	75.00	100.40	94.30	13.4	13.3	23.8	25.6	22.2	25.6	14.9	14.4	21.9	28.6

Average Prices Received by Farmers for Farm Products, June 15, 1940, With Comparisons—Continued

Date	Hogs, per 100 lb.	Beef cattle, per 100 lb.	Veal calves, per 100 lb.	Sheep, per 100 lb.	Lambs, per 100 lb.	Wool, per lb.	Milk cows, per head	Horses, per head	Mules, per head	Loose hay, per ton: All hay, per ton	Loose hay, per ton: Alfalfa	Loose hay, per ton: Clover and timothy mixed	Loose hay, per ton: Prairie	Seed, per bushel: Alfalfa	Seed, per bushel: Red clover	Seed, per bushel: Timothy	Soybeans, per bushel	Cowpeas, per bushel	Peanuts, per lb.
	Dol.	Dol.	Dol.	Dol.	Dol.	Ct.	Dol.	Dol.	Dol.	Dol.	Dol.	Dol.	Dol.	Dol.	Dol.	Dol.	Dol.	Dol.	Ct.
5-year average, August 1909 to July 1914	7.22	5.21	6.75	4.53	5.87	18.3	48.00	136.60	-------	11.87	-------	-------	-------	-------	9.13	-------	-------	-------	4.8
June average, 1910–14	7.16	5.44	6.77	4.75	6.30	17.5	49.60	138.90	-------	12.16	-------	-------	-------	-------	9.09	-------	-------	-------	5.2
1936, June 15	8.91	5.99	7.46	4.03	8.33	27.8	53.80	98.80	112.40	7.31	7.82	8.38	4.75	8.32	9.78	1.28	0.85	1.96	3.28
1937, June 15	9.97	7.13	8.01	4.52	8.88	31.4	57.30	96.50	117.10	10.93	11.76	12.50	7.32	14.48	17.30	2.25	1.50	1.97	4.19
1938, June 15	8.00	6.38	7.73	3.43	6.84	18.0	56.80	86.30	104.80	7.48	8.32	8.64	4.91	15.28	17.75	1.26	.86	1.69	3.49
1939, June 15	5.96	6.81	7.98	3.67	7.49	21.9	57.20	81.30	100.40	6.63	7.40	7.58	4.08	11.89	8.71	1.36	.83	1.59	3.43
July 15	6.26	6.66	8.11	3.66	7.31	21.8	57.20	80.20	99.20	6.76	7.48	7.59	3.93	11.63	8.67	1.41	.75	1.52	3.38
Aug. 15	5.47	6.50	8.13	3.59	6.94	22.0	56.50	78.00	97.00	6.77	7.45	8.00	4.09	10.75	8.55	1.58	.64	1.35	3.39
Sept. 15	7.06	7.07	8.92	3.80	7.57	24.3	58.90	79.90	98.80	7.17	8.04	8.33	4.46	10.58	8.76	1.64	.73	1.28	3.44
Oct. 15	6.52	6.97	8.88	3.92	7.60	28.7	59.40	78.60	97.70	7.31	8.36	8.76	4.68	10.16	8.77	1.59	.73	1.18	3.36
Nov. 15	5.87	6.89	8.64	3.83	7.48	27.6	59.20	77.60	96.60	7.51	8.65	9.08	4.67	10.12	8.59	1.62	.82	1.18	3.39
Dec. 15	5.03	6.85	8.41	3.79	7.38	27.5	59.90	77.10	97.20	7.71	9.01	9.44	4.79	10.17	8.51	1.66	.97	1.22	3.43
1940, Jan. 15	5.18	6.94	8.95	3.86	7.57	28.1	59.90	78.30	98.10	7.90	9.21	9.74	4.89	10.29	8.75	1.81	1.01	1.28	3.56
Feb. 15	4.97	6.84	8.80	3.93	7.61	27.8	60.40	78.20	97.30	8.10	9.38	10.02	4.80	10.54	8.95	1.96	.96	1.35	3.60
Mar. 15	4.87	7.00	8.81	4.25	8.05	27.3	60.40	78.20	97.70	8.22	9.34	10.21	4.87	11.04	8.88	2.08	1.01	1.41	3.60
Apr. 15	4.90	7.16	8.63	4.15	8.14	26.1	60.40	76.60	95.90	8.29	9.14	10.20	4.83	11.18	8.96	2.11	1.00	1.47	3.53
May	5.35	7.35	8.91	4.02	8.25	27.6	61.00	76.10	96.10	8.32	8.92	10.35	4.72	11.23	8.88	2.04	.96	1.52	3.66
June	4.82	7.10	8.46	3.81	8.12	28.6	61.10	75.00	94.30	7.71	8.07	9.57	4.43	10.75	8.62	1.87	.79	1.51	3.52

Average Prices Received by Farmers for Farm Products, June 15, 1939 and 1940, by States—Continued

State and division	Hay (loose), per ton						Seed, per bushel							
	Alfalfa		Clover and timothy mixed		Prairie		Alfalfa		Red clover		Sweet clover		Timothy	
	1939	1940	1939	1940	1939	1940	1939	1940	1939	1940	1939	1940	1939	1940
	Dol.	Dol.	Dol.	Dol.	Dol.	Dol.	Dol.	Dol.	Dol.	Dol.	Dol.	Dol.	Dol.	Dol.
Me	12.00	14.00	7.80	8.90	4.20	4.50								
N. H	14.00	17.00	10.80	15.00	6.00	6.50								
Vt	12.00	15.50	9.00	11.30	5.00	6.50								
Mass	18.00	21.00	15.00	18.50	8.00	9.50								
R. I	19.00	21.00	15.00	18.00	8.00	9.50								
Conn	18.00	21.00	15.50	18.80	8.00	9.00								
N. E	15.67	18.80	10.94	13.31	6.24	7.20								
N. Y	10.00	16.10	7.60	13.30	3.50	8.00			10.50	12.00				
N. J	16.10	20.20	14.80	18.10	7.00	7.00								
Pa	13.20	18.10	10.30	15.00	5.50	8.50			10.80	11.30			2.35	2.65
M. A.	11.81	17.34	8.79	14.08	4.50	7.81			10.64	11.46				
Ohio	6.70	7.00	6.00	6.50	3.00	4.00	15.50	10.60	8.55	8.35	4.00	2.80	1.30	1.80
Ind	7.00	7.80	6.10	7.50	3.80	5.00	15.00	12.50	8.20	8.30	4.00	4.00	1.55	2.10
Ill	6.70	7.70	5.50	7.10	4.10	4.60			8.70	8.10	3.50	4.00	1.45	1.85
Mich	7.10	8.80	6.50	7.30	4.30	4.50	14.00	11.80	7.60	7.80	3.75	2.50		2.80
Wis	9.00	10.20	7.00	7.60	4.40	3.80	15.40	12.30	9.00	7.90	3.28	2.35	1.70	1.60
E.N.C.	7.72	8.63	6.31	7.22	4.34	3.88	14.60	11.76	8.32	8.09	3.80	3.44	1.46	1.88
Minn	5.20	5.70	3.80	5.40	3.20	3.20	14.40	11.60	10.80	9.50	3.20	3.00	1.25	1.50
Iowa	6.90	7.80	5.60	6.80	4.60	5.20	14.90	13.70	10.70	10.00	4.00	3.10	1.35	1.95
Mo	7.70	7.90	7.10	7.10	5.10	5.00			9.90	8.80	3.50	3.40	1.30	1.70
N. Dak.	5.90	4.75	4.30	3.90	3.50	3.10	14.60	11.40			3.50	3.10		
S. Dak.	6.30	6.40	4.50	4.50	3.30	2.50	15.40	12.00			3.30	2.90		
Nebr.	5.50	7.80	4.50	7.00	3.00	4.60	12.60	12.30	11.00	11.00	3.80	3.50		
Kans	6.50	7.10	5.10	6.50	2.90	4.00	11.50	10.80	12.00	9.90	3.30	2.80		
W.N.C.	6.00	6.85	5.49	6.23	3.26	3.71	12.86	11.57	10.49	9.73	3.84	3.00	1.33	1.86
Del	14.00	18.00	11.80	16.50	8.00	9.00								
Md	12.00	14.40	10.50	12.90	8.00	9.00			9.30	10.70				
Va	13.00	14.70	11.10	12.90	8.00	8.00			10.00	11.00				
W. Va.	11.70	14.10	9.70	10.30	7.00	8.00								
N. C.	17.00	17.00	12.70	15.90	8.60	10.00								
S. C.	17.60	16.00	15.00	9.00										
Ga.	15.50	17.50	15.00	15.50	10.00	9.50								
Fla			8.80	10.00										
S. A.	12.08	14.88	10.60	12.42	8.48	9.30			9.39	10.73				
Ky	10.00	10.80	8.90	10.80	4.50	5.00			12.00	10.80				
Tenn	11.40	15.30	10.70	13.50	5.50	6.00								
Ala	13.30	16.40	11.00	14.50	8.20	9.20								
Miss	10.50	10.80	11.00	11.90	8.10	7.90								
E.S.C.	10.44	11.69	9.57	12.44	7.06	7.28								
Ark	8.80	9.30	9.20	9.00	6.20	6.00								
La	11.00	12.00			6.00	6.60								
Okla	7.40	8.00			4.40	5.40	9.80	8.40						
Tex	10.20	10.60			7.60	7.90	9.00	8.20						
W.S.C.	8.50	9.17			5.64	6.24	9.78	8.38						
Mont.	4.90	4.60	4.00	4.50	4.50	4.00	13.50	11.40			3.15	2.85		
Idaho	6.00	7.20	6.00	8.00	6.00	5.00	13.00	13.00	8.50	7.50				
Wyo	6.50	7.60	6.50	6.00	6.20	5.60	12.00	11.00			3.30	2.80		
Colo	6.50	7.80	6.30	7.70	5.30	6.10	12.00	12.80			3.40	3.10		
N. Mex.	8.00	10.50	7.50	9.00	7.50	9.00	9.90	8.30						
Ariz.	7.70	8.00			7.50	7.00	9.00	9.90	8.30					
Utah	7.90	9.30	6.80	9.00	6.30	6.00	12.00	12.00						
Nev.	7.30	7.30	6.80	8.00	4.50	5.00								
Mount	6.49	7.32	5.54	5.92	5.18	4.98	11.69	10.80			3.21	2.88		
Wash.	8.30	7.30	8.60	7.10	6.80	6.00			12.70				8.40	
Oreg.	8.40	7.00	8.50	7.70	6.10	5.00	13.50	12.00	8.10	8.40				
Calif.	8.30	6.80	7.60	7.00	6.50	5.20	11.30	8.50						
Pac.	8.31	6.91	8.42	7.21	6.32	5.16	10.96	9.21			8.42			
U. S.	7.40	8.07	7.58	9.57	4.08	4.43	11.89	10.75	8.71	8.32	3.39	3.06	1.36	1.87

¹ Revised.

Average Wage Rates Paid to Hired Farm Labor, by States, July 1, 1939 and 1940

State and division	Per month, with board		Per month, without board		Per day, with board		Per day, without board	
	1939	1940	1939	1940	1939	1940	1939	1940
	Dol.	Dol.	Dol.	Dol.	Dol.	Dol.	Dol.	Dol.
Maine	33.00	32.00	45.50	49.75	1.60	1.65	2.25	2.30
New Hampshire	31.00	31.25	55.00	54.00	2.15	1.95	3.00	2.85
Vermont	31.25	32.50	48.25	48.75	1.75	1.80	2.45	2.70
Massachusetts	32.00	34.00	61.75	62.20	1.95	1.75	2.85	2.70
Rhode Island	40.00	36.25	65.50	63.00	2.20	2.05	3.05	2.70
Connecticut	35.25	36.75	65.00	63.25	1.85	2.00	2.90	2.90
New England	32.96	33.91	57.24	57.90	1.79	1.80	2.71	2.67

Average Wage Rates Paid to Hired Farm Labor, by States, July 1 1939 and 1940

State and division	Per month, with board		Per month, without board		Per day, with board		Per day, without board	
	1939	1940	1939	1940	1939	1940	1939	1940
	Dol.	Dol.	Dol.	Dol.	Dol.	Dol.	Dol.	Dol.
New York	30.50	32.50	46.00	48.25	1.75	1.80	2.35	2.40
New Jersey	32.50	34.50	54.25	56.50	1.85	1.90	2.50	2.55
Pennsylvania	26.75	27.75	42.00	43.00	1.70	1.75	2.25	2.30
Middle Atlantic	29.23	30.73	45.56	47.13	1.74	1.79	2.33	2.38
Ohio	26.75	27.00	39.50	39.50	1.70	1.65	2.15	2.15
Indiana	27.75	28.50	37.75	39.25	1.55	1.60	1.95	2.00
Illinois	33.00	33.50	43.50	43.75	1.75	1.80	2.25	2.30
Michigan	29.00	30.25	43.50	43.75	1.70	1.75	2.25	2.25
Wisconsin	30.00	31.25	43.00	44.00	1.55	1.55	2.05	2.10
East North Central	29.57	30.35	41.71	42.25	1.66	1.68	2.15	2.17
Minnesota	32.25	32.75	43.75	44.25	1.70	1.65	2.35	2.30
Iowa	34.25	34.25	43.50	44.00	1.85	1.85	2.35	2.35
Missouri	34.00	23.75	33.00	32.50	1.20	1.20	1.50	1.55
North Dakota	29.25	31.50	43.00	44.50	1.30	1.40	1.95	2.20
South Dakota	29.25	30.00	41.50	42.75	1.40	1.45	2.00	2.00
Nebraska	27.00	27.50	36.50	37.50	1.45	1.40	1.95	1.90
Kansas	25.75	26.25	37.00	37.00	1.75	1.55	2.15	2.15
West North Central	29.05	29.37	39.19	39.67	1.57	1.53	2.06	2.06
Delaware	25.00	26.50	38.00	39.75	1.50	1.45	1.90	2.00
Maryland	27.50	28.25	39.50	40.25	1.45	1.50	1.95	1.95
Virginia	20.50	21.75	30.75	31.00	1.10	1.10	1.45	1.50
West Virginia	21.75	22.50	32.00	33.00	1.00	1.05	1.50	1.50
North Carolina	16.75	17.00	24.75	25.00	.95	.95	1.20	1.20
South Carolina	12.50	12.75	18.75	18.75	.60	.65	.80	.85
Georgia	12.25	13.25	18.25	19.00	.70	.70	.90	.90
Florida	15.50	16.00	26.50	28.25	.85	.85	1.25	1.25
South Atlantic	16.89	17.55	25.17	25.69	.99	.92	1.20	1.21
Kentucky	21.25	20.50	30.00	29.00	1.00	1.00	1.30	1.30
Tennessee	16.75	17.00	24.50	24.50	.80	.85	1.05	1.05
Alabama	14.00	13.50	19.75	19.50	.70	.65	.90	.85
Mississippi	14.50	14.75	21.00	21.25	.75	.75	.95	1.00
East South Central	16.47	16.14	23.57	23.21	.81	.80	1.04	1.04
Arkansas	16.50	16.75	24.25	24.25	.80	.80	1.05	1.05
Louisiana	15.25	15.50	22.75	23.25	.80	.80	1.05	1.05
Oklahoma	21.00	21.50	30.50	31.00	1.25	1.20	1.55	1.50
Texas	26.75	21.75	29.50	30.25	1.05	1.05	1.30	1.30
West South Central	19.10	19.87	27.68	28.25	1.00	1.00	1.26	1.26
Montana	39.50	41.25	55.75	57.50	1.90	1.95	2.60	2.70
Idaho	39.50	41.25	54.50	56.25	1.90	2.10	2.50	2.60
Wyoming	37.50	38.00	54.00	54.50	1.60	1.70	2.30	2.35
Colorado	30.75	31.75	46.75	47.25	1.50	1.55	2.10	2.15
New Mexico	28.00	27.75	40.50	40.75	1.25	1.30	1.65	1.65
Arizona	39.75	36.75	57.00	57.00	1.70	1.80	2.10	2.10
Utah	44.50	46.75	58.50	60.75	2.30	2.25	2.60	2.65
Nevada	46.00	44.00	66.75	60.00	2.00	2.00	2.80	2.80
Mountain	37.24	36.91	53.64	52.43	1.75	1.74	2.34	2.29
Washington	37.00	39.00	55.00	59.00	1.95	2.15	2.60	2.85
Oregon	37.50	38.75	54.50	55.75	1.90	2.00	2.45	2.50
California	46.50	45.50	69.50	72.00	2.05	2.10	2.80	2.85
Pacific	43.18	42.34	64.04	65.12	2.00	2.09	2.70	2.77
United States	28.18	29.01	36.26	37.18	1.36	1.37	1.59	1.62

Farm Wage Rates and Index Numbers, 1940, With Comparisons

Year	Farm wage rates				Weighted average rate per month¹	Index numbers of farm wage rates (1910–14=100)
	Per month—		Per day—			
	With board	Without board	With board	Without board		
1935	22.42	30.24	1.07	1.33	25.53	103
1936	24.43	32.28	1.15	1.42	27.51	111
1937	28.00	36.32	1.33	1.64	31.25	126
1938	27.72	35.63	1.31	1.58	30.61	124
1939	27.47	35.85	1.30	1.56	30.61	124
1939:						
January	24.86	34.92	1.20	1.53	29.08	117
April	27.08	35.42	1.23	1.53	30.03	121
July	28.18	36.26	1.36	1.59	31.23	126
October	28.28	36.13	1.35	1.57	31.13	126
1940:						
January	25.33	35.27	1.22	1.55	29.40	119
April	27.45	36.41	1.26	1.55	30.60	124
July	29.01	37.18	1.37	1.62	31.94	129

¹ This column has significance only as an essential step in computing the wage rate index.

Pig Crop Report, June 1, 1940

Hog production is now declining, having reached the peak of the production cycle in 1939. The 1940 pig crop will be materially smaller than that of 1939, but will be larger than for any other year since 1933.

The spring pig crop of 1940 is estimated as 8 percent smaller than that of 1939. The number of sows to farrow in the fall season of 1940 is indicated as 12 percent smaller. The total number of sows to farrow in 1940—spring and fall—is indicated as about 8 percent smaller and, with litters averaging somewhat smaller this year, the total pig crop will probably be down about 10 percent. Compared with the 10-year (1929-38) average, the pig crop this year will be about 7 percent larger; but compared with the 10-year (1924-33) predrought average it will be about 3 percent smaller.

State and division	Pigs saved							
	Spring (Dec. 1 to June 1)						Fall (June 1 to Dec.)	
	Number		1940		Average number per litter			Number
	10-yr. av. 1929-38	1939	Per-cent of 1939	Num-ber	10-yr. av. 1929-38	1939	1940	10-yr. av. 1929-38	1939

State and division	10-yr. av. 1929-38	1939	Per-cent of 1939	Num-ber	10-yr. av. 1929-38	1939	1940	10-yr. av. 1929-38	1939
	1,000	*1,000*		*1,000*				*1,000*	*1,000*
Maine	34	45	80	36	6.2	6.2	6.4	32	37
New Hampshire	12	14	93	13	6.8	5.9	6.0	8	10
Vermont	22	21	95	20	6.7	6.1	6.5	23	30
Massachusetts	84	87	84	73	5.4	6.3	6.2	67	80
Rhode Island	5	6	100	6	6.1	5.9	6.2	4	7
Connecticut	17	17	82	14	6.2	5.5	5.3	17	20
New York	143	221	86	191	6.6	6.9	6.6	138	168
New Jersey	64	90	89	80	5.9	6.0	5.7	46	60
Pennsylvania	336	420	97	409	6.4	6.0	6.1	361	489
North Atlantic	717	921	91	842	6.23	6.14	6.08	696	901
Ohio	2,204	2,602	96	2,499	6.58	6.49	6.17	1,904	2,473
Indiana	2,711	3,371	100	3,364	6.30	6.36	6.05	2,147	2,891
Illinois	3,926	4,560	99	4,492	6.08	6.08	5.99	2,279	2,966
Michigan	616	799	102	817	6.70	6.44	6.38	479	583
Wisconsin	1,693	2,067	102	2,102	6.46	6.50	6.61	820	1,163
East North Central	11,150	13,399	99	13,274	6.30	6.31	6.15	7,629	10,079
Minnesota	3,718	4,310	99	4,283	6.01	6.21	6.19	1,100	1,193
Iowa	9,518	10,548	94	10,050	5.92	6.05	6.08	3,222	3,710
Missouri	2,568	2,614	94	2,450	6.26	6.33	6.05	2,049	2,285
North Dakota	755	787	101	791	6.00	6.45	6.48	330	101
South Dakota	2,073	1,884	97	1,833	5.84	6.30	6.13	388	317
Nebraska	3,696	3,877	80	2,484	5.76	6.13	6.03	1,129	948
Kansas	1,542	1,376	80	1,096	6.08	6.34	6.16	1,165	1,082
West North Central	23,870	24,696	93	22,927	5.94	6.16	6.11	9,183	9,616
North Central	35,020	38,095	95	36,201	8.05	6.21	6.13	16,812	19,695
Delaware	15	22	96	21	6.1	6.2	6.3	13	20
Maryland	117	179	89	159	6.0	6.4	6.1	126	191
Virginia	420	525	83	438	6.3	6.4	6.0	423	598
West Virginia	144	172	81	139	6.7	6.9	6.6	151	189
North Carolina	580	817	87	714	5.8	6.1	5.9	499	614
South Carolina	336	564	79	445	5.5	5.7	5.3	273	394
Georgia	885	1,187	75	890	5.7	5.6	5.3	696	774
Florida	320	427	80	342	5.1	5.4	5.1	288	302
South Atlantic	2,817	3,893	81	3,148	5.88	5.89	2,419	3,192	
Kentucky	686	920	83	762	6.3	6.3	6.0	645	931
Tennessee	646	949	75	714	6.1	6.2	5.9	592	826
Alabama	585	751	77	576	5.4	5.4	5.1	434	594
Mississippi	502	700	79	550	5.4	5.3	5.0	420	594
Arkansas	606	1,115	79	885	5.3	5.6	5.6	503	793
Louisiana	551	755	92	676	5.1	4.9	4.9	411	629
Oklahoma	627	887	75	661	5.9	6.2	5.8	578	863
Texas	1,089	1,392	82	1,142	5.6	5.8	5.6	915	1,368
South Central	5,192	7,449	80	5,966	5.68	5.77	5.50	4,498	6,668
Montana	166	165	108	178	6.2	6.6	6.6	104	112
Idaho	247	346	98	338	6.1	6.4	6.5	135	198
Wyoming	64	63	90	57	5.5	5.8	5.9	26	64
Colorado	282	283	76	216	5.6	5.9	6.0	211	222
New Mexico	51	67	94	63	5.5	5.6	5.7	38	64
Arizona	20	35	100	35	5.5	5.3	5.9	10	12
Utah	82	101	83	84	5.9	6.3	6.3	52	73
Nevada	15	23	96	22	6.6	6.1	5.9	11	12
Washington	162	218	96	210	6.6	6.8	7.0	127	170
Oregon	167	203	98	198	6.6	6.7	7.0	134	182
California	383	484	93	451	5.6	5.9	5.9	376	487
Western	1,609	1,985	93	1,860	5.92	6.24	6.18	1,210	1,529
United States	45,355	52,343	92	48,007	5.97	6.12	6.01	25,635	31,985

State and division	Sows farrowed							
	Spring (Dec. 1 to June 1)				Fall (June 1 to Dec. 1)			
	Number		1940		Number		1940 [1]	
	10-yr. av. 1929-38	1939	Per-cent of 1939	Num-ber	10-yr. av. 1929-38	1939	Per-cent of 1939	Num-ber
	1,000	*1,000*		*1,000*	*1,000*	*1,000*		*1,000*
Maine	6	7	79	6	5	5	91	5
New Hampshire	2	2	92	2	1	2	94	2
Vermont	3	3	91	3	3	4	85	4
Massachusetts	16	16	88	14	11	14	82	11
Rhode Island	1	1	90	1	1	1	91	1
Connecticut	3	3	84	3	3	3	85	3
New York	22	32	91	29	20	24	92	22
New Jersey	11	15	93	14	8	10	92	9
Pennsylvania	53	70	96	67	56	73	86	63
North Atlantic	117	149	92	139	108	136	87	120
Ohio	338	401	101	405	288	368	95	350
Indiana	432	530	105	556	338	438	98	429
Illinois	648	750	100	750	368	454	97	440
Michigan	92	124	103	128	71	100	90	90
Wisconsin	262	318	100	318	125	169	96	162
East North Central	1,772	2,123	102	2,157	1,190	1,529	96	1,471
Minnesota	622	694	99	687	186	190	100	190
Iowa	1,615	1,780	94	1,653	542	588	94	553
Missouri	414	412	98	405	330	351	90	316
North Dakota	128	122	100	122	23	16	94	15
South Dakota	361	299	100	299	70	52	92	48
Nebraska	657	502	81	407	197	158	78	123
Kansas	259	217	82	178	191	171	70	120
West North Central	4,056	4,007	94	3,751	1,538	1,526	89	1,365
North Central	5,828	6,130	96	5,908	2,728	3,055	93	2,836
Delaware	3	4	97	3	2	3	84	3
Maryland	20	28	93	26	20	29	86	25
Virginia	66	82	89	73	65	77	87	67
West Virginia	21	25	84	21	22	27	81	22
North Carolina	99	134	90	121	83	99	87	86
South Carolina	61	99	85	84	48	68	76	52
Georgia	156	212	79	168	123	177	75	130
Florida	63	79	85	67	48	56	91	51
South Atlantic	489	663	85	563	411	536	81	436
Kentucky	109	146	87	127	100	141	85	120
Tennessee	105	153	79	121	93	129	82	106
Alabama	98	139	81	113	80	124	74	92
Mississippi	93	132	83	110	76	108	83	108
Arkansas	109	189	84	158	88	130	83	108
Louisiana	108	150	92	138	79	121	89	108
Oklahoma	107	143	84	116	97	137	80	110
Texas	184	240	85	204	160	223	75	167
South Central	913	1,292	84	1,085	773	1,111	81	899
Montana	27	25	108	27	17	17	71	12
Idaho	40	54	96	52	23	30	80	24
Wyoming	12	11	90	10	4	3	77	2
Colorado	51	48	75	36	36	37	70	26
New Mexico	9	12	92	11	7	11	82	9
Arizona	4	6	109	6	2	3	91	2
Utah	15	18	88	14	6	11	66	8
Nevada	3	4	100	4	2	3	100	2
Washington	25	30	94	30	18	24	83	20
Oregon	25	29	97	28	20	23	87	20
California	69	82	100	82	66	84	95	80
Western	274	319	94	300	201	244	84	205
United States	7,621	8,553	93	7,995	4,221	5,082	88	4,496

[1] Number indicated to farrow from breeding intentions reports.

The June pig crop report is based upon about 166,000 reports obtained from farmers in cooperation with the Post Office Department through the rural mail carriers.

The number of pigs saved in the spring season of 1940 (December 1, 1939, to June 1, 1940) is estimated at 48,007,000 head. This is a decrease of 4,336,000 head or 8 percent from the spring crop of 1939, but is about 6 percent larger than the 10-year (1929-38) average. The spring pig crop was smaller this year in all regions and in nearly all States. By regions the decreases were: North Atlantic, 9 percent; East North Central, 1 percent; West North Central, 7 percent; South Atlantic, 19 percent; South Central, 20 percent; Western, 7 percent.

The number of sows that farrowed in the spring season of 1940, estimated at 7,995,000 head, was about 7 percent smaller than in 1939. In the Corn Belt States the number was down about 4 percent. The December 1939 pig crop report indicated that on the basis of reported breeding intentions, spring farrowings would be about the same in 1940 as in 1939 for the United States and would be up about 2 percent in the Corn Belt States.

The average number of pigs saved per litter in the spring season of 1940 was below the average in the spring of 1939 and was the smallest in the last 4 years. The average this year was 6.01 for the United States, compared with 6.12 in 1939 and with 6.36 in 1938, which was the largest on record. Compared with last year the average was down rather sharply in some of the Eastern Corn Belt States and in nearly all of the Southern States. This, doubtless, was a result of the unusually low temperatures experienced in most of these States during the late winter and early spring. Farrowings this spring were relatively early with the proportion of sows that farrowed by the end of March in the Corn Belt about the same as last year.

The number of sows to farrow in the fall season of 1940 (June 1 to December 1) is indicated as 4,496,000—a decrease of 585,000 head or about 12 percent. Smaller numbers are indicated for all regions, with decreases as follows: North Atlantic, 13 percent; East North Central, 4 percent; West North Central, 11 percent; South Atlantic, 19 percent; South Central, 19 percent; Western, 16 percent. These decreases are based upon breeding intentions reported about June 1 and upon the assumption that the relationship between breeding intentions and subsequent farrowings will be similar to the relationship in other years of low hog prices and low hog-corn ratios.

Hens and Pullets per Farm Flock [1]

[First day of each month]

Area and year	Jan.	Feb.	Mar.	Apr.	May	June	July	Aug.	Sept.	Oct.	Nov.	Dec.
NORTH ATLANTIC												
10-year average, 1929–38	94.9	94.9	93.0	90.0	85.9	82.4	77.4	75.1	73.6	80.4	87.6	93.9
1939	98.4	96.5	94.2	89.1	84.2	80.5	75.4	73.3	70.7	78.6	88.5	92.9
1940	97.2	94.8	92.9	88.2	84.2	80.2	74.2					
E. N. CENTRAL												
10-year average, 1929–38	108.8	107.7	104.5	101.7	96.4	90.3	83.8	79.5	77.7	83.8	93.1	108.1
1939	107.3	106.7	103.4	100.3	93.2	87.9	81.6	76.7	77.6	85.3	98.0	107.4
1940	110.8	109.3	105.6	101.7	97.3	91.3	83.5					
W. N. CENTRAL												
10-year average, 1929–38	118.8	118.3	114.0	112.7	106.8	99.8	91.8	85.5	83.2	90.8	98.6	109.6
1939	113.1	113.2	110.3	107.5	102.6	95.1	87.4	81.7	80.5	87.3	98.7	109.9
1940	118.6	116.9	118.1	113.6	109.5	102.4	92.1					
SOUTH ATLANTIC												
10-year average, 1929–38	58.9	57.6	56.2	53.9	50.4	48.2	46.9	45.6	46.2	49.8	52.6	55.8
1939	59.9	57.7	56.2	53.1	49.4	48.1	45.9	44.0	46.5	50.3	54.8	56.9
1940	59.9	58.8	58.7	56.8	53.3	51.2	47.1					
SOUTH CENTRAL												
10-year average, 1929–38	65.0	64.4	62.2	58.8	54.4	51.4	49.4	49.0	49.5	54.7	57.4	60.6
1939	63.6	63.4	61.6	59.0	55.2	52.9	50.8	49.0	50.8	56.4	59.3	62.4
1940	65.8	64.0	62.9	59.9	56.5	52.6	49.4					
WESTERN												
10-year average, 1929–38	73.2	72.7	70.9	68.6	66.4	63.5	60.4	59.3	58.8	61.4	66.8	71.0
1939	73.6	71.1	69.0	67.1	62.9	60.3	57.7	56.9	56.8	62.2	67.5	70.4
1940	73.7	71.6	69.7	67.4	64.4	62.4	58.9					
UNITED STATES												
10-year average, 1929–38	84.5	83.6	81.0	78.4	73.9	69.7	65.6	63.1	62.5	67.9	73.3	79.4
1939	82.8	82.0	79.8	76.8	72.2	68.5	64.3	61.3	62.1	68.0	75.1	80.8
1940	85.1	83.6	82.6	79.0	75.3	70.8	65.3					

[1] As reported in the returns of flocks by about 20,000 crop correspondents, excluding flocks numbering 400 or more hens and pullets of laying age on Jan. 1. Figures for the last month are preliminary.

Index of Farm Prices of Eggs, Chickens, and Feed for Poultry

[1921–30 average for same month=100]

Item	1939								1940					
	Apr.	May	June	July	Aug.	Sept.	Oct.	Nov.	Dec.	Jan.	Feb.	Mar.	Apr.	May	June
Eggs	71	69	68	70	68	68	64	59	46	47	65	66	69	69	65
Chickens	68	64	63	65	64	67	64	66	64	61	60	62	61	63	62
Feed for poultry	63	65	64	61	57	69	67	72	75	75	75	75	78	78	74

Eggs Laid Daily Per Farm Flock

Area and year	Jan.	Feb.	Mar.	Apr.	May	June	July	Aug.	Sept.	Oct.	Nov.	Dec.
NORTH ATLANTIC												
10-year average, 1929–38	25.1	31.2	38.9	50.2	51.0	45.1	37.5	33.6	28.7	22.8	17.8	20.4
1939	32.3	36.4	45.4	51.4	50.2	42.5	37.9	34.2	29.6	26.1	24.0	26.2
1940	33.1	33.3	43.9	48.7	49.6	45.9	37.8					
E. N. CENTRAL												
10-year average, 1929–38	21.2	28.6	38.9	55.3	56.6	47.9	38.1	31.6	27.8	22.2	16.8	16.8
1939	28.4	34.6	43.0	56.2	55.2	48.2	39.4	32.9	29.3	24.2	22.3	26.2
1940	32.0	28.6	43.9	53.8	56.9	51.0	40.1					
W. N. CENTRAL												
10-year average, 1929–38	17.4	24.9	38.5	58.4	59.9	50.4	38.6	30.4	26.4	22.0	15.1	12.7
1939	24.2	32.6	39.0	59.7	60.2	50.6	40.4	31.9	28.6	22.1	17.7	19.8
1940	27.6	22.3	42.5	58.9	64.2	55.2	42.6					
SOUTH ATLANTIC												
10-year average, 1929–38	12.2	17.0	23.6	28.0	25.5	21.9	18.9	16.5	14.0	12.4	10.8	10.5
1939	15.5	19.1	26.4	28.9	26.2	23.2	19.1	16.8	15.4	14.5	13.7	13.7
1940	16.7	14.6	26.2	29.5	27.7	24.7	20.0					
SOUTH CENTRAL												
10-year average, 1929–38	11.6	16.9	25.7	31.2	28.0	23.2	19.0	16.2	13.7	13.2	11.6	9.9
1939	14.4	19.1	27.0	32.8	29.6	25.3	20.6	17.2	15.8	13.7	13.0	11.8
1940	14.8	12.1	24.7	32.1	29.8	24.9	20.7					
WESTERN												
10-year average, 1929–38	16.4	21.3	30.6	38.8	39.3	34.8	29.6	26.4	23.0	18.9	14.8	13.2
1939	19.6	26.0	29.6	39.3	37.4	32.6	28.1	25.7	22.7	19.8	17.0	16.1
1940	21.8	21.6	32.3	39.5	38.1	33.8	28.6					
UNITED STATES												
10-year average, 1929–38	15.8	21.8	31.3	41.8	41.0	34.8	28.0	23.5	20.3	17.4	13.7	12.7
1939	20.4	26.0	33.3	42.9	41.1	35.3	29.0	24.4	21.7	18.5	16.6	17.3
1940	22.2	19.4	33.4	42.1	42.5	37.1	29.8					

Hog and Corn Ratios, 1918–40

The Curve Shows the Number of Bushels of Corn Equal in Value to 100 Pounds o Live Hogs at Average Farm Prices

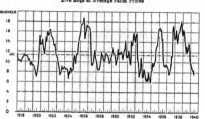

Hog-Corn Ratios, 1928–40

Number of Bushels of Corn Required to Buy 100 Pounds of Live Hogs, Based on Averages of Farm Prices of Corn and Hogs for the Month

Year	Jan. 15	Feb. 15	Mar. 15	Apr. 15	May 15	June 15	July 15	Aug. 15	Sept. 15	Oct. 15	Nov. 15	Dec. 15	Average
	Bu.	Bu.	Bu.	Bu.	Bu.	Bu.	Bu.	Bu.	Bu.	Bu.	Bu.	Bu.	Bu.
1928	10.4	9.6	8.7	8.4	8.6	8.5	9.4	10.2	11.7	11.3	10.4	10.4	9.9
1929	10.2	10.2	11.8	11.7	11.6	11.3	11.3	10.7	9.8	9.9	10.8	10.9	10.8
1930	11.4	12.2	12.8	11.7	11.6	11.5	10.9	9.8	10.3	10.7	12.4	11.5	11.4
1931	11.8	11.6	12.0	12.0	11.3	10.6	11.5	12.8	12.6	14.1	11.9	10.9	11.9
1932	11.2	10.9	12.1	11.4	9.8	9.4	14.1	13.4	13.5	15.0	15.7	14.5	12.6
1933	7.0	15.2	15.6	11.4	10.0	9.9	7.2	7.8	8.0	10.7	9.1	7.0	10.3
1934	7.0	8.5	8.2	7.4	6.5	6.3	6.7	6.3	7.8	6.8	6.7	6.0	7.0
1935	8.1	8.4	9.8	9.2	9.3	10.0	10.2	12.6	13.2	13.8	15.1	16.5	11.3
1936	16.7	16.8	16.8	16.4	14.3	14.5	11.4	9.6	9.2	9.4	9.2	9.5	12.8
1937	9.3	8.9	8.7	7.6	7.7	8.5	9.1	11.2	21.2	16.6	17.2	15.8	11.0
1938	14.5	15.0	16.3	14.7	13.0	15.3	15.9	16.1	16.8	17.4	15.1	15.0	15.8
1939	15.4	16.4	18.0	14.5	13.2	11.9	13.1	12.0	12.6	13.7	12.5	10.0	13.4
1940	9.7	9.1	8.7	8.4	8.4	7.8							

Livestock–Meats–Wool

Weights and Prices of Stocker and Feeder Steers at Chicago, Kansas City, and South St, Paul

June 1940, With Comparisons

Weight range	Number of head			Percent of total by weight ranges			Average weight			Average price per 100 pounds		
	June 1940	May 1940	June 1939	June 1940	May 1940	June 1939	June 1940	May 1940	June 1939	June 1940	May 1940	June 1939
Chicago							Lb.	Lb.	Lb.	Dol.	Dol.	Dol.
1,001 lb. up...	49	32	107	1.1	0.7	2.6	1,071	1,151	1,048	9.96	9.16	8.45
901–1,000 lb...	406	270	335	9.5	6.0	8.1	944	932	948	9.15	9.44	8.77
801–900 lb...	546	707	551	12.7	15.6	13.3	840	845	836	8.98	9.05	8.68
701–800 lb...	883	1,348	906	20.6	29.7	21.8	752	751	747	8.84	9.34	8.52
501–700 lb...	2,408	2,176	2,250	56.1	48.0	54.2	600	609	603	9.04	9.33	8.35
Total....	4,292	4,533	4,149	100.0	100.0	100.0	700	711	705	9.02	9.29	8.50
Kansas City												
1,001 lb. up...	240	269	518	3.0	2.9	5.0	1,115	1,056	1,043	8.53	9.12	7.55
901–1,000 lb...	319	352	734	4.0	4.1	7.1	965	936	933	7.86	8.66	7.74
801–900 lb...	1,078	744	1,544	13.6	8.0	14.9	842	848	832	7.67	9.18	7.97
701–800 lb...	1,411	1,401	1,627	17.7	15.0	15.8	717	751	751	7.99	9.18	7.77
501–700 lb...	4,905	6,541	5,911	61.7	70.0	57.2	591	594	599	8.17	9.23	8.07
Total....	7,953	9,337	10,334	100.0	100.0	100.0	678	666	704	8.05	9.18	7.94
South St. Paul												
1,001 lb. up...	13	108	.....	.4	2.3	.....	1,087	1,101	.....	8.49	9.06	.....
901–1,000 lb...	102	302	89	3.5	6.8	2.5	965	932	922	7.75	7.88	7.06
801–900 lb...	224	594	246	7.7	12.9	6.8	846	855	843	7.17	7.55	7.51
701–800 lb...	536	1,153	753	18.6	25.1	20.9	751	741	754	8.18	8.21	7.69
501–700 lb...	2,021	2,438	2,512	69.8	53.1	69.8	593	617	601	7.84	8.14	7.58
Total....	2,896	4,595	3,600	100.0	100.0	100.0	657	711	658	7.85	8.08	7.58

Beef Steers Sold Out of First Hands at Chicago for Slaughter

June 1940, With Comparisons

Grade	Number of head			Percent of total by grades			Average weight			Average price per 100 pounds		
	June 1940	May 1940	June 1939	June 1940	May 1940	June 1939	June 1940	May 1940	June 1939	June 1940	May 1940	June 1939
							Lb.	Lb.	Lb.	Dol.	Dol.	Dol.
Choice and Prime...	24,872	17,282	13,378	32.2	20.7	17.2	1,182	1,201	1,210	10.32	10.69	10.03
Good...	36,181	39,907	42,740	46.9	47.7	55.0	1,035	1,073	1,058	9.57	9.92	9.29
Medium...	14,981	25,132	18,965	19.4	27.7	24.4	933	965	944	8.84	9.05	8.54
Common...	1,119	3,285	2,607	1.5	3.9	3.4	812	852	913	7.69	8.22	7.67
Total....	77,153	83,606	77,690	100.0	100.0	100.0	1,060	1,061	1,052	9.69	9.83	9.22

Statistical Report of the Livestock and Meat Situation, May 1940, With Comparisons

Item	May		Percentage May 1940 of—		January–May		Percentage 5 months 1940 of—	
	1940	1939	May 1939	5-year average	1940	1939	5 months 1939	5 months, 5-year average
Number slaughtered under Federal inspection (thousands of head):								
Cattle...	796	814	98	108	3,833	3,679	104	100
Calves...	501	509	98	97	2,215	2,244	99	93
Hogs...	3,890	3,416	114	101	21,114	15,510	128	149
Sheep and lambs...	1,420	1,392	102	100	6,951	6,906	101	99
Average live weight (pounds):								
Cattle...	945.12	935.64			954.93	942.64		
Steers [1]...	986.23	967.58			174.57	174.56		
Calves...	168.82	179.80			232.27	232.84		
Hogs...	283.07	235.84			89.43	89.99		
Sheep and lambs...	83.40	83.80						

Statistical Report of the Livestock and Meat Situation, May 1940, With Comparisons—Continued

Item	May		Percentage May 1940 of—		January–May		Percentage 5 months 1940 of—	
	1940	1939	May 1939	5-year average	1940	1939	5 months 1939	5 months, 5-year average
Total live weight (thousands of pounds):								
Cattle...	752,133	761,259	99	106	3,660,449	3,467,858	106	104
Calves...	84,553	91,519	92	94	386,662	391,769	99	92
Hogs...	906,685	805,573	113	103	4,904,227	3,844,052	128	152
Sheep and lambs...	118,444	116,658	102	100	621,895	621,464	100	101
Total [2]...	1,861,815	1,775,010	105	123	9,573,144	8,325,174	115	123
Average cost to packers (dollars per 100 pounds):								
Cattle...	8.30	7.98	105	109	7.82	7.91	99	109
Steers [1]...	9.36	9.18						
Calves...	9.38	8.52	110	119	9.02	8.76	103	115
Hogs...	5.64	6.62	85	66	5.30	7.17	74	61
Sheep and lambs...	9.04	8.94	101	106	9.05	8.75	103	103
Total cost to packers (thousands of dollars):								
Cattle...	62,427	60,368	103	116	286,190	274,473	104	113
Calves...	7,931	7,797	102	112	34,858	34,314	102	106
Hogs...	51,137	53,329	96	101	259,793	275,713	94	93
Sheep and lambs...	10,707	10,429	103	106	56,284	54,402	103	104
Total [2]...	132,202	131,923	100	109	637,126	638,903	100	103
Dressing yields (per 100 pounds live weight):								
Cattle...	55.95	54.80			55.31	54.24		
Calves...	57.85	56.34			56.68	56.48		
Hogs...	74.73	75.33			75.01	75.58		
Sheep and lambs...	47.85	47.58			46.95	46.63		
Lard...	13.99	13.31			14.23	13.58		
Average dressed weight (pounds):								
Cattle...	528.77	512.71			528.16	511.29		
Calves...	97.67	101.30			98.94	98.59		
Hogs...	174.18	177.66			174.23	175.98		
Sheep and lambs...	39.91	39.87			42.00	41.96		
Condemnations (number of head):								
Cattle...	4,515	4,421			22,178	21,692		
Calves...	1,538	1,407			10,279	5,206		
Hogs...	9,471	7,690			50,732	40,307		
Sheep and lambs...	2,827	2,633			15,172	12,799		
Total dressed weight—excluding condemned (thousands of pounds):								
Beef...	418,411	414,886	101	109	2,012,834	1,869,885	108	107
Veal...	48,768	51,420	95	95	218,137	220,351	99	91
Pork and lard...	673,942	605,478	112	151	3,669,988	2,898,284	127	152
Lamb and mutton...	56,567	55,398	102	100	291,314	289,214	101	101
Total [2]...	1,199,688	1,127,182	106	128	6,192,273	5,277,735	117	128
Lard production...	126,550	106,945	118	167	696,414	520,816	134	172
Apparent consumption—total (thousands of pounds, dressed weight basis):								
Beef and veal...	484,142	478,116	101	106	2,282,527	2,143,783	106	103
Pork and lard...	659,459	570,476	116	140	3,250,729	2,683,820	123	142
Lamb and mutton...	56,647	55,539	102	99	292,336	290,782	101	101
Total [2]...	1,200,248	1,105,132	109	122	5,825,592	5,068,385	115	122
Lard...	93,776	71,839	131	158	467,069	370,905	126	156
Apparent consumption—per capita (pounds):								
Beef and veal...	3.67	3.66	100	104	17.32	16.38	106	101
Pork and lard...	5.00	4.35	115	137	24.66	20.11	123	140
Lamb and mutton...	.43	.42	102	98	2.22	2.22	100	99
Total...	9.10	8.43	108	120	44.20	38.71	114	119
Lard...	.71	.55	129	154	3.54	2.84	125	152
Exports (thousands of pounds):								
Beef and veal...	1,366	1,036	132	124	7,274	4,734	154	135
Lamb and mutton...	51	39	129	157	362	205	177	151
Fresh pork...	1,187	1,582	76	183	32,219	7,000	456	733
Cured pork [2]...	2,365	9,164	26	31	32,430	36,635	90	116
Canned pork [2]...	229	962	23	30	4,205	120	132	
Total pork [2]...	3,775	11,687	32	41	69,704	47,300	147	193
Sausage...	220	234	94	112	1,340	1,253	107	118
Sausage ingredients...	167	314	53	80	933	882	106	117
Lard...	14,889	25,303	59	93	107,513	117,996	91	149
Imports (thousands of pounds):								
Beef and veal...	9,502	11,630	82	100	35,051	34,752	101	96
Pork...	685	4,820	14	18	2,907	22,894	13	16
Lamb and mutton...	14		92	292	44	23	191	126

[1] Steers also included with cattle.   [2] Totals based on unrounded numbers.

Receipts and Disposition of Livestock at Public Stockyards for June

[65 Markets]

Stockyard	Cattle (excluding calves)								Calves							
	Receipts		Local slaughter		Stocker and feeder shipments		Total shipments		Receipts		Local slaughter		Stocker and feeder shipments		Total shipments	
	1940	1939	1940	1939	1940	1939	1940	1939	1940	1939	1940	1939	1940	1939	1940	1939
Atlanta, Ga.	555	420	378	535	133	----	176	----		497						497
Baltimore, Md.	7,218	7,974	4,831	5,265	1,097	778	2,387	2,719	4,059	5,159	3,095	3,872			964	1,287
Birmingham, Ala.	790	604	701	527	97	74	97	74	163	238	163	238				
Boston, Mass.	3,823	3,827	(¹)		(¹)		(¹)		5,650	5,587	(¹)		(¹)	(¹)	(¹)	(¹)
Buffalo, N.Y.	13,762	12,737	7,375	7,864	193	154	6,404	5,046	21,705	17,892	5,209	4,691			16,500	13,229
Bushnell, Ill.	302	516			109	38	296	427	80	189		42	30	52	78	152
Chattanooga ²	3,695	3,421	2,875	2,401	1,120	1,020	1,120	1,020								
Cheyenne, Wyo.¹	113	246						113	246							
Chicago, Ill.	144,805	142,199	98,898	99,282	7,875	6,134	46,108	42,947	21,887	26,872	20,545	22,277	(¹)	(¹)	1,042	1,295
Cincinnati, Ohio	15,845	15,396	12,785	13,623	608	567	3,070	1,773	10,075	9,173	7,899	7,451			2,176	1,722
Cleveland, Ohio	8,146	8,284	7,637	7,764	157	210	809	520	10,178	11,255	9,443	10,530	16		735	726
Dayton, Ohio	1,402	1,287	968	1,287			434		925	755	757	755			168	
Denver, Colo.	21,827	25,687	13,754	16,220	3,985	4,045	8,930	9,856	4,022	4,041	2,412	3,104	1,581	903	1,630	908
Detroit, Mich.	14,617	13,795	12,518	13,707	1,880	1,915	2,031	2,088	13,295	14,576	9,687	12,554			3,808	2,020
El Paso, Tex.	6,895	6,280	2,851	1,839	2,905	5,144	4,044	4,441	4,123	2,039		189	4,029	1,693	4,123	1,850
Evansville, Ind.	2,777	3,796	2,437	2,956	282	473	336	899	3,288	3,175	2,886	3,104	86	71	397	71
Fort Wayne, Ind.	1,992	1,410	1,902	1,410					1,694	839					1,594	839
Fort Worth, Tex.	40,534	53,345	16,434	22,906	8,880	16,778	17,403	19,944	24,494	33,403	9,167	12,857	12,779	13,183	22,025	31,009
Houston, Tex.	9,939	7,768	4,810	4,198	567	128	2,139	3,611	21,969	20,307	11,478	9,590	9,584	5,944	10,494	10,747
Indianapolis, Ind.	23,188	23,001	13,209	10,452	2,148	3,872	10,120	12,574	15,787	15,635	5,065	8,278	1,646	984	10,722	8,357
Jersey City, N.J.	16,414	17,489	16,414	17,479				10	44,943	42,349	41,602	42,299				50
Joplin, Mo.	3,500	4,002	714	809	1,840	1,087	2,786	3,193	3,273	3,713	53	96	732	690	3,220	3,617
Kansas City, Mo.	68,220	67,436	33,103	40,362	25,854	22,554	33,825	30,425	19,938	18,120	8,095	9,329	9,584	7,105	11,606	9,021
Knoxville, Tenn.	3,258	2,688	1,042	1,212	1,216	874	1,216	874	2,767	2,646	2,767	2,648		21		
LaFayette, Ind.	235	163	96	86	33	12	150	85	681	433	8	21	12	36	676	411
Lancaster, Pa.	19,228	17,460	74	407	6,674	3,200	19,154	17,053	4,279	4,255	220	168			4,059	4,087
Laredo, Tex.	1,301	700	50				1,251	700		90						90
Los Angeles, Calif.	18,087	19,144	16,554	17,894	1,708	2,118	1,798	2,118	8,673	5,205	4,184	5,226	186	137	186	187
Louisville, Ky.	8,443	6,422	4,552	4,501	8,922	6,667	3,791	1,621	13,896	13,138	2,079	2,451	(¹)	(¹)	11,819	10,687
Memphis, Tenn.	10,689	10,944	8,445	9,812	2,211	2,422	4,309	3,316	5,390	5,424	2,121	2,708	214	20	1,061	343
Milwaukee, Wis.	11,470	13,847	11,331	13,164	42	86	165	648	24,374	23,924	24,374	23,924				
Montgomery, Ala.	4,993	6,778	3,805	4,452	805	1,095	1,258	1,895	2,436	3,105	1,312	2,838	28	22	1,070	146
Muncie, Ind.	697	910	600	763			92	138	850	932	283	361			667	571
Nashville, Tenn.	4,216	5,890	2,671	4,176	819	1,164	1,974	1,714	31,717	33,187	3,872	3,585			345	298
Nat'l. Stk. Yards, Ill.	64,671	56,873	34,094	33,543	8,107	5,891	30,907	23,130	40,376	41,014	21,840	24,807			18,536	16,207
New Orleans, La.	4,122	4,429	1,293	1,043	567	1,093	2,848	3,466	6,176	5,174	5,271	8,066	250		733	
New York, N.Y.	1,688	1,421	1,688	1,421					14,117	10,356	14,117	10,356				
North Salt Lake, Utah	5,736	5,048	1,678	1,385	200	200	4,030	3,534	241	304	241	304				
Ogden, Utah	5,538	5,256	2,819	1,272	1,299	1,600	3,177	3,985	104	760	691	139	436	365	430	619
Oklahoma City, Okla.	27,602	30,663	7,463	14,738	12,954	4,594	20,838	17,226	12,228	14,383	6,763	9,157	5,346	896	5,466	5,335
Omaha, Nebr.	87,337	87,481	61,552	61,755	10,271	6,842	26,065	25,726	4,904	4,869	3,581	2,733	1,323	2,078	1,323	2,136
Parsons, Kans.	2,599	1,753	198	263	980	534	2,401	1,490	1,654	1,501	41	70	461	269	1,613	1,431
Pasco, Wash.	600	247					600		43						43	
Peoria, Ill.	6,291	6,365	3,802	3,955	651	363	2,487	2,533	4,706	4,227	2,418	3,008	192	193	1,624	1,335
Philadelphia, Pa.	3,089	3,163	2,985	3,142			104	21	5,855	5,857	5,863	5,844				13
Pittsburgh, Pa.	25,508	20,068	8,224	7,925			17,284	12,141	23,821	25,252	6,243	7,210			22,878	18,042
Portland, Oreg.	12,170	11,911	8,618	8,111	815	554	3,469	3,812	1,476	1,986	1,405	1,494	25		71	492
Pueblo, Colo.	259	1,642			536	1,495		132	87			47			47	
Richmond, Va.	1,424	1,269	972	1,137	402	106	452	132	1,837	1,836	1,837	1,836				
St. Joseph, Mo.	20,251	19,063	14,288	14,849	4,417	2,901	6,206	5,280	4,518	4,674	3,403	3,704	1,252	958	1,282	1,009
St. Louis, Mo.	1,782	1,530	1,623	1,565	108	93	108	108	787	970	787	970				
San Antonio, Tex.	11,328	11,791	6,341	7,406	2,543	2,212	4,940	4,483	16,832	24,977	5,358	7,280	6,091	4,306	11,402	17,731
Seattle, Wash.	2,805	2,617	2,715	2,483	90	34	90	34	270	1,797	260	1,797	10		10	
Sioux City, Iowa	56,765	51,300	34,603	32,144	6,528	5,009	22,162	19,150	2,529	2,653	1,090	3,025	1,439	1,637	1,439	1,637
Sioux Falls, S. Dak.	15,261	12,926	6,959	7,475	3,109	2,101	8,353	6,382	603	715	65	137	372	484	541	671
So. St. Paul, Minn.	68,195	64,337	43,176	43,808	9,134	9,656	24,977	20,474	37,304	40,328	26,138	34,855	1,029	914	10,995	5,133
So. San Francisco	6,116	6,859	4,763	5,079	239	361	1,286	1,780	1,315	1,191	1,273	1,174			37	17
Spokane, Wash.	5,749	4,741	3,629	2,932	1,273	1,445	2,558	1,967	874	714	770	597	168	168	198	168
Springfield, Ill.	384	376	225	159	30	21	154	224	726	700	577	599	100	97	141	97
Springfield, Mo.	3,276	3,559	509	426	390	620	2,767	3,133	7,881	8,793	280	578	720	1,575	7,601	8,215
Stockton, Calif.	1,454	1,350			58	122	1,620	1,422	1,281	819	1,455			40	1,676	1,455
Toledo, Ohio	2,507	2,608	1,265	1,776	362		1,281	819	437	477	437	477				433
Tulsa, Okla.	3,899	3,502	1,412	1,415	1,889	1,005	2,487	2,087	4,057	3,427	180	241	1,674	1,106	3,907	3,216
West Fargo, N. Dak.	11,452	11,887	435	1,200	4,469	4,756	10,967	10,619	1,953	2,912	7		1,366	1,409	1,782	3,155
Wichita, Kans.	13,819	12,562	6,850	8,422	4,216	3,913	5,414	4,329	3,048	2,486	2,339	2,248	1,915	1,218	1,979	1,222
Discontinued markets		2,738		2,561		44		44		1,709						
Total	962,783	958,245	566,884	599,994	155,627	138,205	387,505	352,406	498,745	517,560	291,343	327,677	60,213	48,703	206,490	194,038
Increase or decrease	+4,538		-33,110		+17,422		+35,099		-18,844		-36,334		+11,610		+12,452	
Percentage	+0.5		-5.5		+12.6		+10.0		-3.6		-11.1		+23.6		+6.4	
Total for 6 months ended with June	5,934,870	6,138,019	3,678,966	3,693,298	974,196	1,066,113	2,201,493	2,358,569	2,828,313	3,017,170	1,790,308	1,905,731	326,151	319,630	1,087,714	1,104,641
Increase or decrease	-203,149		-14,332		-91,927		-157,076		-188,857		-185,423		+6,821		-16,927	
Percentage	-3.3		-0.4		-8.6		-6.7		-6.8		-9.7		+2.0		-1.5	
June average, 5 years, 1935-39	1,087,107		662,423		155,960		414,045		549,854		366,992		31,427		179,584	
Increase or decrease	-124,324		-95,539		-333		-26,540		-44,108		-75,649		+28,786		+26,906	
Percentage	-11.4		-14.4		-0.2		-6.4		-8.1		-20.6		+91.6		+15.0	
Drive-ins	682,769	672,192							318,244	328,872						
Percentage of total receipts	70.9	70.1							63.8	63.5						

¹ Disposition of stock not reported.　　² Calves included with cattle.

NOTE.—This report represents the total livestock movements at the specified stockyards, including through shipments. Direct shipments to packers are included only when such shipments pass through the stockyards.

Receipts and Disposition of Livestock at Public Stockyards for June—Continued

[85 Markets]

Stockyard	Hogs Receipts 1940	1939	Local slaughter 1940	1939	Stocker and feeder shipments 1940	1939	Total shipments 1940	1939	Sheep and lambs Receipts 1940	1939	Local slaughter 1940	1939	Stocker and feeder shipments 1940	1939	Total shipments 1940	1939
Atlanta, Ga	2,506	303	106				2,447	303								
Baltimore, Md	35,924	33,446	26,253	23,854			9,671	9,862	14,005	19,809	6,504	9,333	23	47	7,501	10,476
Birmingham, Ala	252	326	178	303	76	29	76	29		18		18				
Boston, Mass	5,380	6,906	(1)	(1)	(1)	(1)	(1)	(1)	57	112	(1)	(1)	(1)	(1)	(1)	(1)
Buffalo, N.Y.	23,110	18,309	6,721	3,380	12	128	16,774	9,547	25,053	28,273	13,881	12,013	104	144	10,890	16,959
Bushnell, Ill.	6,451	7,194	5	40	387	648	6,443	7,147	178	181	3	7	42	28	171	184
Chattanooga, Tenn.	3,871	2,628	3,871	2,628					207	390	207	390				
Cheyenne, Wyo.	12,518	5,563					12,518	5,563	4,506	1,798					4,506	1,798
Chicago, Ill.	442,883	329,970	413,773	290,360	45	465	29,110	39,610	118,485	113,917	113,491	106,668	2,549	3,722	4,994	7,249
Cincinnati, Ohio	91,110	81,912	79,910	67,988	254	300	11,200	13,924	44,573	58,823	29,850	44,910	1,980	218	14,723	13,413
Cleveland, Ohio	24,746	25,344	20,859	24,202		82	3,887	1,142	14,408	11,434	9,706	9,972	325	610	4,702	1,462
Dayton, Ohio	8,464	7,666	3,421	3,262			5,043	4,404	1,911	2,482	1,043	292			868	2,190
Denver, Colo.	44,164	27,453	29,958	24,103	3	15	14,109	3,758	143,346	149,040	24,257	25,252	5,949	19,315	122,868	122,225
Detroit, Mich.	20,039	18,045	17,914	16,737	656	805	2,124	1,508	12,269	17,110	11,984	15,499	202	678	285	1,617
El Paso, Tex.	2,864	4,124	259	2,145	2,605	1,978	2,605	1,978	76	6,997	76	199		4,451		6,798
Evansville, Ind	26,083	29,191	24,565	22,857	685	826	1,547	5,369	5,451	6,379	5,168	5,573	131	117	287	798
Fort Wayne, Ind	18,109	6,547					18,109	6,547	984	553					984	553
Fort Worth, Tex	23,217	27,196	24,484	21,562	356	389	3,731	5,599	152,896	186,490	102,725	79,538	32,478	40,471	50,531	62,558
Houston, Tex.	608	543	608	543					194	761	194	142				619
Indianapolis, Ind.	213,869	157,530	122,241	84,482	680	965	91,633	73,134	11,572	20,551	7,786	9,290	872	541	3,786	11,361
Jersey City, N.J.	20,114	17,867	19,463	17,867			651		119,576	120,025	119,341	119,470			235	555
Joplin, Mo.	9,004	9,901	1,810	2,005	2,625	3,176	7,194	7,896	5,791	6,228	20	21	313	587	5,771	6,202
Kansas City, Mo.	52,787	35,698	44,267	30,376	1,696	2,400	8,329	5,726	105,717	91,472	81,428	77,804	14,755	8,138	25,899	14,235
Knoxville, Tenn.	4,968	4,353	4,968	4,353					1,605	1,641	1,605	1,641				
La Fayette, Ind.	14,068	7,871	695	561	1	6	13,406	7,325	1,060	447	5	26	30	15	1,061	433
Lancaster, Pa.	8,577	7,752	412	108			8,165	7,644	2,868	3,131	305	41			2,563	3,090
Laredo, Tex.																
Los Angeles, Calif.	10,639	6,853	10,501	6,844	259	204	250	204	8,838	13,864	8,098	13,305	565	145	565	145
Louisville, Ky.	29,067	26,571	12,815	15,894	437	532	16,252	12,677	42,266	46,250	1,136	1,860	3,539	3,550	41,162	47,390
Memphis, Tenn.	9,162	11,405	5,871	6,552	787	2,952	806	3,881	369	1,452	293	183	21	1,100	21	1,100
Milwaukee, Wis.	32,767	27,553	32,680	26,984	160	395	160	559	4,397	4,454	4,383	4,427	14	27	14	27
Montgomery, Ala.	2,305	2,302	782	1,535	98	266	1,578	947	757	856	551	465	14	206	14	206
Muncie, Ind.	9,853	6,983	6,350	6,321			3,607	1,802	1,023	1,306	142	108		19	872	1,199
Nashville, Tenn.	9,442	12,813	8,574	6,846			868	5,967	26,056	29,453	7,859	3,489	600		20,597	25,994
Natl. Stock Yds., Ill.	265,043	209,013	177,505	151,720	2,035	2,887	87,424	58,496	122,160	109,342	72,382	70,459	3,206	4,716	49,778	38,284
New Orleans, La.	1,148	1,664	1,051	1,207	239	428	239	496	78	84	30		35	41	35	85
New York, N.Y.	70,991	69,815	70,991	69,815			66,005	28,370	4,990	9,798	4,990	9,798			15,149	25,788
North Salt Lake, Utah	69,229	32,886	3,892	2,987	300	406	16,252	8,391	12,887	28,432	1,325	1,643	4,500	14,000	186,312	174,593
Ogden, Utah	20,410	13,506	6,844	5,014	87	65	13,030	8,391	180,469	175,810	1,404	1,300	8,886	5,496	9,225	9,251
Oklahoma City, Okla.	22,794	32,369	14,481	21,352	573	1,386	8,323	11,049	21,983	20,881	12,827	11,971	2,272	4,186		
Omaha, Nebr.	163,220	122,863	137,669	101,951	1,342	913	25,551	20,912	93,977	110,565	71,953	80,914	14,534	14,093	22,024	29,651
Parsons, Kans.	6,478	6,618	210	156	774	537	6,268	6,462	3,640	3,053			169	140	3,640	3,045
Pasco, Wash.	848	36					848	36	71						71	121
Peoria, Ill.	71,298	48,770	16,059	15,899	946	1,153	55,724	33,321	5,009	8,550	1,764	368	872	325	3,237	3,316
Philadelphia, Pa.	31,656	31,413	31,526	30,981			130	432	10,518	13,049	9,759	11,861			759	1,188
Pittsburgh, Pa.	53,224	41,472	48,306	39,413			4,918	2,059	71,772	60,003	7,357	10,522			64,415	49,381
Portland, Oreg.	20,055	20,217	14,996	15,277	285	363	5,015	4,958	21,965	16,952	14,325	12,266	2,081		7,785	4,736
Seattle, Wash.	267	127					127	140	1,497	2,232			4,896		140	4,896
Richmond, Va.	14,969	16,462	14,953	16,375	16	87	16	87	2,353	986	2,296	933	10	53	56	53
St. Joseph, Mo.	86,766	63,055	80,513	56,883	1,321	1,308	6,182	6,103	24,745	67,267	55,644	59,279	8,236	8,349	9,647	8,349
St. Louis, Mo.	13,507	12,860	8,284	9,075	393	400	5,223	4,281	3,817	9,316	942	1,787			1,847	2,828
San Antonio, Tex.	6,079	10,443	5,428	6,664		1,765	648	3,786	5,394	5,368	2,700	2,758	1,272	1,145	2,633	2,689
Seattle, Wash.	7,831	7,355	7,304	7,391	27	64	27	64	4,343	4,238	4,342	4,238			1	
Sioux City, Iowa	142,716	89,472	119,144	62,500	4,815	4,539	23,872	26,872	42,852	37,728	29,325	27,092	11,727	5,717	13,527	10,651
Sioux Falls, S. Dak.	39,172	33,499	19,372	25,179	45	61	19,401	7,170	3,280	2,944	1,771	1,887	87	120	1,390	1,126
So. St. Paul, Minn.	197,753	144,487	170,700	107,607	3,088	3,978	26,919	35,567	28,186	23,086	16,914	13,152	1,638	2,493	10,461	8,960
So. San Francisco, Calif.	18,264	18,203	16,831	13,585			1,429	2,618	43,509	38,904	28,539	23,870	1,870	631	15,007	15,103
Spokane, Wash.	5,058	4,154	3,529	2,908	301	390	1,699	1,244	3,412	3,512	1,058	1,282	1,013	1,801	1,674	2,341
Springfield, Ill.	27,256	19,710	592	936	1,117	917	26,735	19,335	744	886		152	55	84	560	455
Springfield, Mo.	17,237	13,694	1,620	600	1,127	760	15,617	13,094	19,743	21,659			45	214	19,743	21,659
Stockton, Calif.	5,238	2,131			61	81	5,126	5,249	6,927	10,147			2,185	5,161	6,488	10,421
Toledo, Ohio	3,679	3,307	1,632	2,122	33	110	2,112	1,224	153	1,520	153	246				1,279
Tulsa, Okla.	5,897	6,326	4,400	2,997	1,274	1,500	1,497	3,329	1,507	1,623			124	101	1,593	1,825
West Fargo, N. Dak.	12,945	10,532	159	942	148	208	12,623	9,915	2,126	925	6	1	2,022	922	1,692	1,401
Wichita, Kans.	25,122	23,830	22,277	20,537	1,255	2,458	2,951	3,204	24,559	20,343	21,675	17,502	2,846	2,922	2,846	4,368
Discontinued markets			27,743		28,187					5,249		5,249				
Total	2,649,525	2,105,112	1,927,463	1,539,193	33,419	43,290	717,851	559,995	1,687,420	1,711,002	915,120	913,289	132,495	166,800	778,849	803,630
Increase or decrease	+544,413		+388,270		−9,871		+157,856		−23,582		+1,831		−34,305		−24,781	
Percentage	+25.9		+25.2		−22.8		+28.2		−1.4		+0.2		−20.6		−3.1	
Total for 6 months ended with June	17,323,339	13,385,407	12,591,797	9,850,597	264,430	259,013	4,695,052	3,486,838	10,158,506	10,713,548	5,795,772	5,945,312	748,924	956,895	4,356,624	4,760,909
Increase or decrease	+3,937,932		+2,741,200		+5,417		+1,208,214		−554,742		−149,540		−207,971		−404,285	
Percentage	+29.4		+27.8		+2.1		+34.7		−5.2		−2.5		−21.7		−8.5	
June average, 5 years, 1935-39	1,707,926		1,227,543		34,800		475,916		1,874,362		1,002,828		132,045		870,245	
Increase or decrease	+941,599		+699,920		−1,381		+241,935		−186,942		−87,708		+450		−91,396	
Percentage	+55.1		+57.0		−4.0		+50.8		−10.0		−8.7		+0.3		−10.5	
Drive-ins	1,850,976	1,507,161							680,511	675,218						
Percentage of total receipts	69.9	71.6							40.3	39.5						

[1] Disposition of stock not reported.

NOTE.—This report represents the total livestock movements at the specified stockyards, including through shipments. Direct shipments to packers are included only when such shipments pass through the stockyards.

Receipts and Disposition of Livestock at Public Stockyards June 1940, With Comparisons

[Thousands, i. e., 000 omitted]

Class and year	Receipts			Local slaughter			Stocker and feeder			Total shipments		
	June	January to June	Total, calendar year	June	January to June	Total, calendar year	June	January to June	Total, calendar year	June	January to June	Total, calendar year
Cattle only:												
1932...	870	5,412	11,831	548	3,819	6,646	90	617	2,203	323	2,048	5,114
1933...	984	5,297	12,347	621	3,288	7,369	129	726	2,124	358	1,960	4,593
1934...	1,215	6,532	12,679	771	4,163	11,057	124	732	2,176	433	2,286	8,435
1935...	926	6,280	14,986	572	3,783	8,473	124	904	2,891	342	2,298	6,266
1936...	1,201	6,672	15,711	749	4,223	9,382	143	843	2,639	433	2,364	6,188
1937...	1,271	6,679	15,135	744	4,110	8,478	185	987	2,893	510	2,476	6,468
1938...	1,079	6,316	14,076	647	3,840	7,924	190	987	2,949	422	2,407	6,021
1939...	958	6,138	13,896	600	3,693	7,673	138	1,066	3,161	352	2,359	6,048
1940...	963	5,935		567	3,679		156	974		388	2,201	
Calves only:												
1932...	468	2,734	5,501	326	1,934	3,728	15	110	416	138	782	1,733
1933...	464	2,639	5,587	338	1,844	3,817	20	149	423	131	787	1,748
1934...	597	3,240	6,050	454	2,387	5,709	15	142	480	153	883	2,359
1935...	476	2,128	6,518	382	2,182	4,558	27	166	501	152	978	2,171
1936...	563	3,120	6,870	387	2,158	4,631	25	185	568	177	977	2,275
1937...	631	3,369	7,286	440	2,368	4,796	32	199	578	193	1,003	2,826
1938...	527	3,059	6,563	348	2,027	4,014	25	205	586	183	1,022	2,521
1939...	318	3,017	6,560	328	1,906	3,807	49	220	653	194	1,106	2,763
1940...	499	2,828		291	1,790		60	326		206	1,088	
Hogs:												
1932...	2,545	19,371	35,028	1,624	12,973	23,695	26	187	321	918	6,382	11,303
1933...	3,361	18,028	40,377	2,621	13,334	30,472	46	189	398	737	4,666	9,860
1934...	2,684	17,875	33,720	1,934	12,633	23,919	45	225	558	759	5,233	9,778
1935...	1,301	10,368	19,552	952	7,142	13,509	27	171	334	375	3,219	6,025
1936...	1,984	11,391	26,399	1,348	8,283	18,291	36	205	686	512	3,590	8,062
1937...	1,513	11,883	22,666	1,075	8,396	16,004	29	196	382	432	3,460	6,500
1938...	1,757	12,121	24,801	1,249	8,521	17,775	38	225	422	500	3,564	6,956
1939...	2,103	13,385	27,974	1,539	9,551	20,638	43	259	493	560	3,487	7,251
1940...	2,650	17,323		1,927	12,592		33	264		718	4,695	
Sheep:												
1932...	2,435	18,783	29,306	1,338	7,766	15,100	172	696	3,373	1,087	6,023	14,214
1933...	2,091	12,144	27,184	1,167	6,893	13,965	100	593	3,008	912	5,285	13,196
1934...	1,810	10,608	26,136	918	5,582	13,415	115	673	3,361	881	4,733	12,715
1935...	1,994	11,425	25,567	1,037	6,371	12,927	81	678	2,994	961	5,062	12,626
1936...	1,859	10,795	24,652	981	5,937	12,423	106	622	3,795	879	4,828	12,206
1937...	1,879	11,201	24,979	1,022	6,278	12,322	133	614	3,284	852	4,914	12,686
1938...	1,929	11,682	23,598	1,080	6,710	13,018	171	705	3,367	862	4,970	12,558
1939...	1,711	10,714	23,817	913	5,945	11,827	167	957	3,598	804	4,761	11,976
1940...	1,087	10,150		915	5,796		132	749		779	4,357	

[1] Includes animals purchased for Federal Surplus Relief Corporation from June 6, 1934, to Feb. 7, 1935 for cattle and calves, and from Sept. 14 to Dec. 15, 1934 for sheep.
[2] Includes many pigs and sows received for Government account in Emergency Hog Production Control Program from Aug. 22 to Oct. 7, 1933.

Hogs: Average Cost and Weight of Packer and Shipper Purchases [1]

Average Cost per 100 Pounds

Month	Chicago	Nat'l Stock Yards	Kansas City	Omaha	Sioux City	South St. Joseph	South St. Paul	7 mkts. combined	Indianapolis
	Dol.	Dol.	Dol.	Dol.	Dol.	Dol.	Dol.	Dol.	Dol.
All purchases:									
June 1940...	4.98	5.09	4.88	4.67	4.58	4.88	4.63	4.83	5.05
May 1940...	5.59	5.55	5.42	5.24	5.20	5.39	5.34	5.42	5.57
June 1939...	6.34	6.54	6.22	5.82	5.75	6.23	5.56	6.08	6.47
Barrows and gilts:									
June 1940...	5.17	5.17	4.96	4.84	4.77	4.99	5.03	5.16	
May 1940...	5.70	5.63	5.48	5.32	5.26	5.46	5.50	5.52	5.70
June 1939...	6.63	6.54	6.38	6.14	6.11	6.41	6.19	6.44	6.62
Packing sows: [3]									
June 1940...	4.38	4.42	4.13	4.26	4.22	4.12	4.21	4.27	4.18
May 1940...	4.76	4.90	4.57	4.54	4.58	4.70	4.73	4.73	4.51
June 1939...	5.44	5.37	4.91	5.24	5.19	4.95	5.13	5.26	5.32

Average Weight

	Lb.	Lb.	Lb.	Lb.	Lb.	Lb.	Lb.	Lb.	Lb.
All purchases:									
June 1940...	257	225	253	253	263	227	233	249	226
May 1940...	251	229	226	249	253	227	240	243	224
June 1939...	262	225	233	272	277	231	293	259	225
Barrows and gilts:									
June 1940...	234	215	214	230	237	210	234	226	216
May 1940...	239	219	217	241	246	218	232	231	212
June 1939...	236	217	222	243	246	219	240	231	212
Packing sows: [3]									
June 1940...	380	382	383	338	332	371	340	352	404
May 1940...	425	386	395	365	369	387	355	381	407
June 1939...	375	391	395	347	346	391	347	357	423

Packing Sows [3]—Percentage of Total

	Pct.	Pct.	Pct.	Pct.	Pct.	Pct.	Pct.	Pct.	Pct.
June 1940...	16.0	6.0	5.0	21.0	27.0	7.0	37.0	18.0	7.0
May 1940...	7.0	6.0	5.0	6.0	7.0	6.0	15.0	8.0	6.0
June 1939...	18.0	5.0	6.0	23.0	21.0	7.0	30.0	22.0	5.0

[1] Weighted average of all purchases except pigs under 140 pounds, boars, stags, and defective hogs.
[3] Based on packing sows weighed separately. Relatively few weighed with barrows and gilts necessarily included in computations for these classes.

Receipts of Horses and Mules at Public Stockyards, June 1940

Stockyard	1940	1939	Stockyard	1940	1939
Atlanta, Ga...	153	86	New York, N. Y...	27	75
Baltimore, Md...	235	102	North Salt Lake, Utah...	23	63
Buffalo, N. Y...	1,309	947	Ogden, Utah...	328	401
Cheyenne, Wyo...	51	47	Oklahoma City, Okla...	385	4
Chicago, Ill...	1,007	366	Omaha, Nebr...	376	314
Cincinnati, Ohio...	70	70	Pittsburgh, Pa...	1,185	575
Columbia, S. C...	34	65	Portland, Oreg...	20	18
Denver, Colo...	502	194	Pueblo, Colo...		1
Detroit, Mich...	107	85	St. Joseph, Mo...	36	155
El Paso, Tex...	87	139	San Antonio, Tex...	20	153
Fort Worth, Tex...	396	550	Sioux City, Iowa...	427	540
Houston, Tex...		2	South St. Paul, Minn...	442	645
Indianapolis, Ind...		61	Spokane, Wash...	205	183
Jersey City, N. J...	910	25	Springfield, Mo...	40	
Joplin, Mo...	112	129	Stockton, Calif...	28	
Kansas City, Mo...	1,748	1,729	Tulsa, Okla...		
Knoxville, Tenn...			West Fargo, N. Dak...	501	549
Los Angeles, Calif...	51	35	Wichita, Kans...	96	348
Louisville, Ky...	122		All others...	355	176
Memphis, Tenn...	36				
Milwaukee, Wis...	2	64	Total horses and mules...	13,371	11,296
Montgomery, Ala...	2	177	Total horses [1]...	10,424	8,768
Nashville, Tenn...	264	334	Total mules [1]...	2,947	2,528
National Stock Yards...	1,679	1,889			

Accumulated receipts, 6 months:			June average, 5 years, 1935–39:	
Horses and mules...	139,307	172,895	Horses and mules...	16,834
Horses [1]...	86,105	94,028	Horses [1]...	14,285
Mules [1]...	53,202	78,867	Mules [1]...	2,549

[1] Totals for horses and mules separately are partly estimated as a few stockyard companies do not separate horses and mules on their reports.

Animals Slaughtered Under Federal Meat Inspection, June 1940

Swine	Cattle	Calves	Sheep and lambs	Swine
Chicago [1]...	104,270	33,736	148,633	484,073
Denver...	8,873	1,428	23,244	27,246
Kansas City...	41,245	20,290	113,279	160,582
New York [2]...	33,436	64,623	205,580	184,884
Omaha...	62,516	4,038	85,714	155,193
Saint Louis [3]...	37,169	38,077	90,507	284,786
Sioux City...	34,771	933	34,640	130,909
South St. Paul [4]...	59,014	39,605	19,379	209,975
All other stations...	356,680	234,195	646,847	2,247,747
Total:				
June 1940...	737,974	436,897	1,377,823	3,885,395
June 1939...	778,263	448,452	1,401,475	3,185,098
12 months ended June 1940...	9,360,329	5,223,172	17,262,684	46,673,925
12 months ended June 1939...	9,541,238	5,383,503	17,504,256	38,656,537

Slaughter:			Horses	Goats
June 1940...			1,263	121
June 1939...			1,512	140
12 months ended June 1940...			28,178	3,661
12 months ended June 1939...			28,158	4,005

[1] Includes Elburn, Ill.
[2] Includes Jersey City and Newark, N. J
[3] Includes National Stock Yards and East St. Louis, Ill.
[4] Includes Newport and St. Paul, Minn.

Wool: Monthly Average Prices at Boston

June 1940, Compared With Corresponding Month, 1939

[In cents per pound]

Classification	Scoured basis						Grease basis	
	Territory		Semibright fleece		Bright fleece		Bright fleece	
	1940	1939	1940	1939	1940	1939	1940	1939
Fine:								
Combing (staple) [1]...	90.4	70.8	86.0	69.8	88.0	73.5	34.5	29.4
French Combing...	84.5	67.8						
Clothing...	79.9	62.9	79.6	64.2	80.5	65.4	24.5	23.5
½ Blood:								
Combing (staple)...	86.1	67.5	80.6	64.9	82.5	66.9	35.5	29.5
French Combing...	82.9	64.5						
Clothing...	77.6	60.8						
⅜ Blood:								
Combing...	77.1	59.8	73.5	58.0	74.8	58.9	39.5	31.5
Clothing...	72.9	55.8						
¼ Blood: Combing...	72.9	55.8	69.2	56.8	70.4	55.6	39.5	31.5
Low ¼ Blood...	75.1	53.9	67.6	52.5	69.2	53.5	39.5	31.1
Common and Braid...	71.6	51.5			64.6	50.8	37.5	29.2

[1] Delaine in grease wool.

Dairy and Poultry

Stocks, Imports, and Exports of Evaporated, Condensed, and Dry Milk

Stocks June 1, and Imports and Exports during May, With Comparisons

Stocks	June 1, 1940	May 1, 1940 [1]	June 1, 1939 [1]
	1,000 lb.	*1,000 lb.*	*1,000 lb.*
Evaporated (case goods)	287,778	207,740	209,044
Condensed (case goods)	6,815	4,014	6,437
Dry whole milk	4,277	3,107	3,619
Dry skim milk	35,569	33,573	31,982
Dry buttermilk	3,917	3,256	5,394

	May 1940	April 1940	May 1939
IMPORTS	*1,000 lb.*	*1,000 lb.*	*1,000 lb.*
Evaporated milk	0	0	0
Condensed milk	(²)	(²)	15
Dry milk	(²)	(²)	(²)
EXPORTS			
Evaporated milk	3,636	3,878	2,508
Condensed milk	442	361	148
Dry milk	1,003	815	1,069

¹ Revised figures include late reports.   ² Less than 1,000 pounds.

Production of Evaporated and Condensed Milk Reported by Manufacturers, May 1940

Commodity	May 1940 [1]	April 1940 [1]	May 1939 [1]
	1,000 lb.	*1,000 lb.*	*1,000 lb.*
Evaporated (case goods)	281,960	225,077	268,512
Condensed (case goods)	4,906	3,169	2,903

¹ Estimated, subject to revision.

Production of Dry Milk Reported by Manufacturers, May 1940

Includes Reports From Principal Firms Operating Dry Milk Factories in the United States

Classes of dry milk	Comparison of production (pounds) for same firms					
	Previous year			Previous month		
	Firms	May 1940	May 1939	Firms	May 1940	April 1940
Whole milk	19	3,784,281	2,551,574	19	3,784,281	1,926,108
Skim milk	144	42,770,561	39,362,040	149	43,132,966	36,990,380
Cream	2	3,424	0	2	3,424	0
Buttermilk	86	3,506,228	3,517,783	13	3,562,638	3,025,971

Figures showing number of firms do not represent number of factories since some firms operate more than 1 factory.

Prices to Producers at Condenseries for 3.5 Percent Milk

May and April 1940

[In dollars per 100 pounds]

Geographic section	By manufacturers of case goods		
	May 1940	April 1940	May 1939
Middle Atlantic	$1.33	$1.37	$1.11
South Atlantic	1.36	1.42	1.22
East North Central	1.24	1.27	1.10
West North Central	1.22	1.26	1.05
South Central	1.20	1.24	1.03
Western (North)	1.24	1.26	1.05
Western (South)	1.36	1.39	1.12
United States	1.26	1.29	1.10

Wholesale Prices of Evaporated and Condensed Milk

May and April 1940

Geographic section	Unsweetened evaporated milk (per case of 48 14½-ounce cans)		Sweetened condensed milk (per case of 48 14-ounce cans)	
	May	April	May	April
New England	$2.83	$2.87	$4.80	$4.80
Middle Atlantic	2.76	2.82	4.72	4.72
South Atlantic	2.80	2.85	4.72	4.72
East North Central	2.71	2.77	5.25	5.25
West North Central	2.74	2.78	5.25	5.25
South Central	2.79	2.80	4.72	4.72
Western (North)	2.81	2.85		
Western (South)	2.75	2.80		
United States:				
1940	2.77	2.82	4.80	4.80
1939	2.68	2.67	4.80	4.86

Wholesale Selling Prices of Dry Milk During May 1940

[Cents per pound]

Dry skim milk (bulk goods)—reported sales (average price, 5.35)		Dry whole milk (bulk goods)—reported sales (average price, 15.09)		Dry buttermilk (bulk goods)—reported sales (average price, 5.06)	
Price	Pounds	Price	Pounds	Price	Pounds
3–3½	783,865	12– 12½	263,100	3½– 4½	694,065
3½–4	3,027,259	12½–13½		4½– 5½	1,583,674
4–4½	6,809,875	13½–14½	598,456	5½– 6½	678,831
4½–5	4,526,500	14½–15½	167,500	6½– 7½	14,750
5–5½	5,627,717	15½–16½	114,580	7½– 8½	
5½–6	3,996,517	16½–17½	143,511	8½– 9½	1,850
6–6½	13,953,613	17½–18½	292,260	9½–10½	1,925
6½–7	4,688,200	18½–19½	2,600	14½–15	1,200
7–7½	349,770				
7½–8	282,705				
Total	44,085,041		1,582,007		2,976,295

Wholesale prices reported on case goods were as follows: Dry whole milk (1-pound cans), 36.756 cents per pound.

Dealers' Prices for Standard Grade Milk Testing 3.5 Percent Butterfat

Used for City Distribution as Milk and Cream
[Delivered f. o. b. local shipping point or at country plant [1]]

Section	Number of local markets	Range of prices per 100 pounds	Average price	Comparison of prices for same markets			
				Number of local markets	Average for—		
					July 1940	June 1940	July 1940
New England	12	$2.34–$3.16	$2.79	12	$2.79	$2.79	$2.76
Middle Atlantic	16	2.08– 3.00	2.51	16	2.51	2.51	2.21
East North Central	26	1.50– 2.45	1.90	26	1.90	1.90	1.79
West North Central	21	1.30– 2.20	1.84	21	1.84	1.84	1.79
South Atlantic	18	1.50– 3.87	2.70	18	2.70	2.70	2.72
East South Central	6	1.35– 2.55	2.05	6	2.05	2.05	1.93
West South Central	8	1.50– 2.45	1.86	8	1.86	1.86	1.94
Mountain	5	1.60– 2.29	1.81	5	1.81	1.81	1.88
Pacific	11	1.48– 2.34	1.93	10	1.96	1.97	1.86
United States	123	1.30– 3.87	2.18	122	2.18	2.18	2.10

¹ The prices at country points apply to milk delivered direct by farmers in their own cans to local milk shipping stations and nearby city milk plants. "Basic" prices are used for cities where a surplus plan or pooling plan is in effect, and where net prices are not yet determined. The price per 100 pounds may be reduced to cents per quart by dividing by 46.53.

Feed grain production still depends largely upon how favorable the weather is for corn, but judging from conditions on July 1, the combined production of corn, oats, barley, and grain sorghums should be about 94 million tons, or about 3 percent below production in 1938 and 1939. As reductions in the numbers of hogs and chickens are expected to reduce the total units of grain-consuming livestock on the farms about 4 percent during the current year, the prospective production of feed grains would provide the usual utilization of grain per unit without drawing on the large reserves of feed grains now on the farms. The hay crop will be outstanding—probably the largest since 1927.

Report of Fluid Milk Market for July 1940
Wholesale and Retail Milk Prices at Cities

State	City	Dealers' buying price at city for 3.5 percent butterfat[1]	Selling price[2] On routes — Bulk	Selling price[2] On routes — Wholesale trade Bottles	Selling price[2] Family trade Bottles	At retail stores Bottles	Prevailing butter-fat test of milk sold by dealers
		Cents per qt.	Cents per qt.	Cents per qt.	Cents per qt.	Cents per qt.	Percent
Ala.	Birmingham	6.13		12	15	14	4.2–4.5
	Mobile	5.70	10	11.5	14	14	
Ariz.	Phoenix	5.95	8.75	9	12	11	
Calif.	Los Angeles	4.51	6.75	8	11	10	3.5–4.2
	San Francisco	4.81	7.87	9	12	11	3.6–4.0
Colo.	Colo. Springs	3.76	7.5		10	10	3.6–4.0
	Denver	4.30			11–12		
Conn.	Hartford	6.94	10	11	14	13	3.8–4.0
	New Haven	6.94	10	11	14	13	3.9–4.0
Del.	Wilmington	5.52	9	11	12	11–13	4.0
D. C.	Washington	6.94	10	11.5	14	11–14	4.0–4.1
Fla.	Jacksonville	6.98	12	14	16	16	4.0–4.8
	Miami	7.78	12.5	14	16	16	3.2–4.4
	Tampa	5.89	12	13	15	15	4.3–4.4
Ga.	Macon	5.97	10	11	14	13	4.3–4.6
Ill.	Chicago		7.5–8.5	7.5	13	8.5–9	3.5–3.63
Ind.	Quincy	3.89	6.25	8	10	10	4.0
	Evansville	4.05		9.5	11	11	3.6–3.87
	Indianapolis	4.36	7.5	8.5	11	10	3.7–3.8
	South Bend	4.88	8.75	10	12	12	3.7–3.9
Ia.	Burlington	4.30	7.5	8.5	10	10	4.0
	Davenport	4.51	7.5	9	11	11	3.8
	Des Moines	4.30	8	8	11	10	3.7
	Sioux City	4.84	8	9	11	10	3.7
Kans.	Topeka	3.76	7.5	8	10	10	3.8
	Wichita	4.75	9.25	10	12	12	3.5–3.8
Ky.	Lexington	4.08	7.5	9–10	12	11	4.0–4.5
	Louisville		8.5	11	12–13	12	4.0
La.	New Orleans	5.16	8	9	13	11	4.0
	Shreveport	4.41		8	10	10	
Md.	Baltimore	5.70	9	10	13	12	4.0
	Cumberland	7.09	10	11	13	13	4.0–4.2
Mass.	Boston	6.58	9.5–9.75	10.5	13	12	3.7–4.0
	Lowell	6.43			13	12	
	Springfield	6.96	10.5	11	14	13	3.9–4.1
	Worcester	7.46	10.5–11	11	14	13	3.8–3.9
Mich.	Detroit	4.47	7.5	8	11	9	3.7–4.0
	Grand Rapids	4.30–4.41		8	11	10–11	3.5–4.0
	Kalamazoo	5.27	9	10	12	12	4.0
	Lansing	3.65	7.5	7.5	9	9	3.7–3.8
Minn.	Duluth		7	8	9–10		3.8–3.9
	Minneapolis		7.5–7.75	7.5	12	8–10	3.5
	Winona	3.98	6.5	7	9	9	3.8
Mo.	Kansas City	4.51	8–9	8–10	11–12	10–11	3.6–4.0
	St. Louis	4.81	7.5–9.5	10	12.5	10–13	3.5–3.8
Mont.	Butte	5.42	8.25	10	12	12	3.5–3.8
Neb.	Lincoln	3.37	7	7	9	8–9	3.8
	Omaha	4.64	7.5	9	11	10	3.8
N. H.	Manchester	6.08			12	12	
	Portsmouth	5.03	9	10	12	12	3.9
N. J.	Trenton	6.13	10	11.5	13.5	12.5	3.66–3.9
N. Y.	Albany	5.70	8–9	11–13	13	13	4.15–4.3
	Buffalo	5.59	9	10.5	13	12	3.6
	New York	6.44–6.80	9.75	10–12	14.5	11–13½	
	Rochester	5.70	10–11	11.5	14	13–14	3.7
N. C.	Winston-Salem	6.02	10	12.5	15	15	4.2
N. Dak.	Grand Forks	4.30	7.5	8	10	9–10	3.5
Ohio.	Cincinnati	4.62	8	8	10	9	3.7
	Cleveland	3.98			10	9	
	Columbus	3.80	7–7.5	8	10	9	3.5–4.0
	Toledo	5.05			12		
Okla.	Tulsa	5.87	7.65–8	8	11	10	3.8
Oreg.	Portland	4.36	9	9	11	11	4.0
Pa.	Philadelphia	5.97	10	10	12	11–13	
	Pittsburgh	5.37	10–10.5	10.5	12	12	3.7–3.74
	Reading	5.16	9.5	10.5	12	12	3.6
R. I.	Newport			13	15	13	4.3
	Providence	7.37	10.5	11	14	13	3.7–3.9
S. C.	Charleston	6.06	10–11	13	14.5–15	13	4.1
Tenn.	Knoxville	3.44	8.75	9	11	11	4.0
	Memphis	5.27			11	11	
Tex.	Dallas	4.08–4.51	9	9	11	10	4.3–4.5
	El Paso	4.98			10	9–10	
	Houston	5.70			13	11	4.3
Utah.	Salt Lake City	3.76	7.5	7.5	10	9	3.8–3.85
Va.	Richmond	7.48	10.75	13	14	14	4.0
	Roanoke	5.72	10	11	13	13	4.0
Wash.	Seattle	4.21	8	8.5	11	11	4.0
	Spokane	4.61	7.5	9	11	10–11	3.7–4.0
W. Va.	Charleston	6.49		13	15	15	3.7–4.0
	Clarksburg	5.37	8.75	10	12	12	3.6–4.0
	Wheeling	4.51	9	9	11	11	3.7–4.0
Wis.	Beloit	4.30	8	8.5	10	10	3.8
	Madison	5.59	9.5	10	11	11	3.8
	Milwaukee	5.16	8–8.75	9.5	11	11	3.5–3.7
	Racine	5.16	9	9.5	11	11	3.6

[1] Prices paid for milk used in fluid form for city distribution.
[2] These prices represent grade B milk or the grade which is most commonly sold, the butterfat content varying from 3.5 to 4.8 percent in different cities.
[3] Reduced from 4.81 cents on July 8.
[4] Flat price paid for all milk delivered by producers.
[5] Price at country receiving stations.
[6] This price applies to June also.

Creamery Butter Production, by States, May 1940, With Comparisons[1]

State	May 1940	April 1940	May 1939	May average, 1930–38	Change in May 1940 production from— April 1940	Change in May 1940 production from— May 1939	Change in May 1940 production from— May average, 1930–38
	1,000 pounds	1,000 pounds	1,000 pounds	1,000 pounds	Percent	Percent	Percent
Vermont	230	220	335		+35	+5	−31
New York	1,800	2,400	1,465	1,325	−25	+23	+36
Pennsylvania	1,140	680	1,380	1,155	+68	−17	−1
Ohio	7,740	5,090	8,580	8,670	+52	−10	−11
Indiana	7,340	5,010	7,280	7,525	+47	+1	−4
Illinois	8,000	5,700	7,800	7,820	+40	+3	+2
Michigan	9,800	7,760	9,590	8,415	+24		+14
Wisconsin	18,000	15,800	18,160	18,680	+14	−1	−3
Minnesota	32,385	28,150	33,835	30,395	+15	−4	+7
Iowa	25,640	20,040	25,700	24,350	+28		+5
Missouri	8,980	5,300	9,725	10,345	+67	−8	−13
North Dakota	5,850	4,380	5,570	4,610	+34	+5	+27
South Dakota	4,870	3,410	4,700	4,300	+43	+4	+13
Nebraska	8,030	5,645	8,280	9,405	+42	−3	−15
Kansas	8,500	5,900	9,190	8,430	+44	−8	+1
Virginia	585	320	670	580	+83	−13	+1
Kentucky	1,729	980	2,010	2,150	+76	−14	−20
Tennessee	1,380	900	1,765	1,735	+53	−22	−20
Mississippi	450	285	670	815	+58	−33	−45
Oklahoma	5,040	3,280	5,920	4,705	+54	−15	+7
Texas	3,800	2,580	3,330	3,305	+29	−1	−5
Montana	1,525	1,090	1,340	1,450	+40	+14	+5
Idaho	3,800	3,050	3,470	2,965	+25	+10	+27
Colorado	2,410	1,775	2,545	2,255	+36	−5	+6
Utah	1,150	925	1,215	1,085	+24	−5	+6
Washington	4,710	3,640	4,360	4,125	+29	+8	+14
Oregon	4,020	3,285	3,705	3,395	+22	+9	+18
California	7,500	8,030	6,760	7,940	−7	+11	−2
Other States	2,910	2,110	3,195	2,655	+38	−9	+10
United States	188,645	147,745	192,410	184,640	+27.7	−2.0	+2.2

[1] Amounts shown are estimates subject to revision except 1930–38 averages, which are from actual enumerations, and 1939 data for the States indicated by (²).
[2] Preliminary enumeration.

Receipts of Butter at 4 Markets, by State of Origin, June 1940

State of origin	New York	Chicago	Philadelphia	Boston	Total, 4 markets
	Pounds	Pounds	Pounds	Pounds	Pounds
Arkansas	19,152	190,238			209,390
Colorado		68,766			68,766
Delaware			497		497
District of Columbia			36,075		36,075
Illinois	3,192,096	2,383,177	804,494	2,747,103	9,065,870
Indiana	285,523	696,755	41,162	238,585	1,262,025
Iowa	7,665,058	5,003,872	625,029	2,455,087	15,772,026
Kansas	1,108,930	2,592,341	337	69,256	3,770,864
Kentucky		55,383			55,383
Maine				8,804	8,804
Maryland			8,804		8,804
Michigan	833,192	585,659		451,875	1,870,726
Minnesota	9,369,683	3,910,830	3,876,885	1,762,536	18,919,884
Missouri	347,419	840,655	171,892	135,857	1,495,823
Nebraska	1,844,362	1,133,471	789,994	180,622	3,848,369
New Hampshire				52	52
New York	451,058		65,262	341,150	858,470
North Dakota	715,668	210,219	125,080		1,753,964
Ohio	146,523	25,988		115,820	591,331
Oklahoma	56,050	2,177,795	27,458	125,213	2,385,523
Pennsylvania	936	1,168	24,567		26,671
Rhode Island				189	189
South Dakota	341,984	1,027,871		63,429	1,433,284
Tennessee	75,852	15,403	36,289		127,544
Texas	19,266	135,123		20,700	175,089
Vermont				12,387	12,387
Virginia	289,944		86,400		376,344
West Virginia			529		529
Wisconsin	1,266,832	8,165,378	208,640	489,931	10,130,681
Wyoming		9,052			9,052
Total:					
June 1940	27,995,334	29,928,044	6,880,344	9,462,750	74,266,672
June 1939	28,321,080	36,569,236	7,073,121	8,449,738	80,413,175

Wholesale Prices of Butter and Cheese, June 1940
[Cents per pound]

	New York	Chicago	Boston	Philadelphia	San Francisco
Butter:					
92 score	26.90	26.27	27.41	27.38	29.30
91 score	26.46	25.74	27.12	26.80	27.62
90 score	26.18	25.55	26.93	26.24	26.62
89 score		25.29	(¹)	(¹)	
Cheese, single daisies	15.73	14.89	15.95	15.76	15.42

[1] Centralized carlots.   [2] No quotation.   [3] Flats.

Receipts of Cheese at 4 Markets, by State of Origin, June 1940

State of origin	New York	Chicago	Philadelphia	Boston	Total, 4 markets
	Pounds	Pounds	Pounds	Pounds	Pounds
Colorado		2,254			2,254
Illinois	1,107,163	565,304	65,415	1,830	1,739,712
Indiana	58,148	314,663	55,914		428,746
Iowa	2,880	12,360			15,240
Massachusetts				21	21
Michigan		1,098	24,998		26,096
Minnesota	48,226	90,783	19,540		158,549
Missouri	41,900	600			42,500
Nebraska		87			87
New York	693,294	144,008	228	267,015	1,104,535
North Dakota		235			235
Ohio	398,375	315		62,763	461,453
Tennessee			94,039		94,039
Vermont	110,157				110,157
Virginia	7				7
Washington	30,002				30,002
Wisconsin	4,062,260	1,883,561	1,929,245	1,085,930	8,960,996
Canada	9,723		100	464	10,287
Total:					
June 1940	6,562,125	3,015,388	2,189,479	1,418,023	13,185,015
June 1939	6,228,218	2,875,970	2,295,575	1,326,756	12,726,519

Receipts of American Cheese at Wisconsin Warehouses

	1940	Corresponding week in 1939	Corresponding 5-year average weekly receipts [1]
	Pounds	Pounds	Pounds
Week ended June 1	7,860,860	7,865,202	6,987,326
Week ended June 8	8,966,604	8,323,448	7,535,084
Week ended June 15	8,881,374	8,409,573	7,756,336
Week ended June 22	8,729,377	8,667,153	7,825,638
Week ended June 29	8,400,697	8,264,825	7,583,570
Total since January 1	147,914,086	133,670,653	121,674,408

[1] 1935-39 inclusive.

American Cheese Production, May 1940, With Comparisons [1]

Geographic division or State	May 1940	April 1940	May 1939	May average 1930-38	Change in May 1940 production from— April 1940	May 1939	May average 1930-38
	1,000 pounds	1,000 pounds	1,000 pounds	1,000 pounds	Percent	Percent	Percent
New York	4,100	1,625	2,990	3,440	+152	+37	+19
North Atlantic (excluding New York)	395	205	280	295	+93	+41	+34
South Atlantic	75	45	105	90	-67	-29	-17
South Central	5,700	4,000	6,180	4,180	+42	-8	+36
Wisconsin	[2]36,000	[2]26,300	[2]32,450	28,040	+37	+11	+28
East North Central (excluding Wisconsin)	8,890	5,910	7,900	5,440	+50	+13	+63
West North Central	4,950	3,475	4,715	3,400	+42	+5	+46
Mountain	2,020	1,630	1,800	1,570	+24	+12	+29
Pacific	5,550	4,430	5,200	4,190	+25	+9	+35
United States	67,780	47,620	61,620	50,645	+42	+10	+34

[1] Amounts shown are estimates subject to revision except 1930-38 averages which are from actual enumerations and 1939 data for New York indicated by (³).
[2] Preliminary enumeration.
[3] Estimates based on receipts of American cheese at Wisconsin warehouses.

Cold-Storage Holdings of Dairy and Poultry Products at 26 Markets,[1] June 1940

Date	Butter	American cheese	Eggs	Dressed poultry
	Pounds	Pounds	Cases	Pounds
June 1	16,934,156	54,692,492	4,074,542	58,484,968
June 8	24,734,290	57,969,842	4,451,612	58,841,377
June 15	34,174,893	61,700,147	4,792,821	60,889,067
June 22	24,686,013	64,153,164	5,050,493	62,524,106
June 29	55,123,255	66,658,004	5,230,041	63,339,568

[1] New York, Chicago, Philadelphia, Boston, Providence, Buffalo, Syracuse, Cuba (N. Y.), Lowville (N. Y.), Pittsburgh, Cleveland, Detroit, Minneapolis, St. Paul, Milwaukee, Plymouth, Marshfield, Green Bay (Wis.), Denver, Kansas City, St. Louis, Omaha, Portland, Seattle, San Francisco, and Los Angeles.

Receipts of Eggs at 4 Markets, by State of Origin, June 1940

State of origin	New York	Chicago	Philadelphia	Boston	Total, 4 markets
	Cases	Cases	Cases	Cases	Cases
California	616	616	1,200		2,432
Colorado		2,815			2,815
Connecticut	42			3	45
Delaware	1,869		1,714		3,583
District of Columbia	1,112				1,112
Idaho	1,000				1,000
Illinois	26,811	92,945	9,050	5,173	133,962
Indiana	33,640	12,745	841	4,347	51,573
Iowa	183,949	221,176	11,442	38,657	455,224
Kansas	17,476	12,568		1,074	31,118
Kentucky	30	400	5,049		5,479
Maryland	4,638		5,632		10,270
Maine				11,463	11,463
Massachusetts	6			11,111	11,117
Michigan	166	1,664		782	2,612
Minnesota	100,126	149,847	33,804	2,230	286,007
Missouri	7,470	56,181	400	3,540	67,591
Nebraska	2,099	37,573	979	290	40,941
New Hampshire				6,834	6,834
New Jersey	20,981		3,115		24,096
New York	89,730			1,437	91,167
North Carolina			4		4
North Dakota	1,008	8,797	6,559		16,364
Ohio	44,278		10,432	348	55,058
Oregon	5,400			600	6,000
Pennsylvania	56,795		31,685	13	88,493
Rhode Island				21	21
South Carolina					3
South Dakota	4,455	19,091	2,700	1	26,247
Tennessee	191	570	206		967
Utah	17,400		1,000		18,400
Vermont	22			2,038	2,060
Virginia	5,777		1,269		7,046
Washington	12,600				12,600
West Virginia	90		118		208
Wisconsin	14,908	105,126		3	120,041
Parcel post	201	136	116	33	486
Canada	420				420
Total:					
June 1940	655,306	722,253	127,322	89,998	1,594,879
June 1939	614,523	688,891	106,082	103,584	1,513,080

Receipts of Dressed Poultry at 4 Markets, by State of Origin, June 1940

State of origin	New York	Chicago	Philadelphia	Boston	Total, 4 markets
	Pounds	Pounds	Pounds	Pounds	Pounds
Alabama	22				22
Arkansas		24,558			24,558
California	57,632			962	58,594
Colorado	24,703	75		59,210	83,988
Connecticut	23,482			2,010	25,492
Delaware	1,517,415				1,517,415
Florida	1,333	405			1,738
Georgia	2,144				2,144
Idaho			30,316		30,316
Illinois	943,380	255,914	195,082	498,800	1,893,126
Indiana	95,183	26,200	44,827	100,261	267,471
Iowa	1,724,181	1,005,893	457,341	812,705	4,000,120
Kansas	1,019,847	202,101	97,942	381,906	1,701,796
Kentucky	23,320	32,903		36,855	93,078
Maine				115,441	115,441
Maryland	361,846	59,578	11,980		433,404
Massachusetts	636,135			616,425	1,252,560
Michigan	10,113			28,142	38,255
Minnesota	991,220	864,125	278,973	335,387	2,469,705
Missouri	994,660	380,984	264,380	236,542	1,876,566
Nebraska	939,971	346,898	185,830	424,335	1,900,034
New Hampshire	249,970			165,853	415,823
New Jersey	416,256		114,193	240	530,689
New York	4,839,940	30,848		75,098	4,970,788
North Carolina	1,509				1,509
North Dakota		31,168	44,359	75,098	150,625
Ohio	254,216		3,124		257,694
Oklahoma	234,370	125,372	77,365	18,953	456,062
Oregon	166,462				166,462
Pennsylvania	750,903		141,283	60	892,196
Rhode Island				86	86
South Carolina	717				717
South Dakota	176,163	111,081	21,253	43,100	352,497
Tennessee	93,367	7,012			100,379
Texas	250,334	141,506	63,275	88,174	543,289
Utah	44,799			37,248	82,047
Vermont	1,634			3,618	5,252
Virginia	278,715		23,941		302,656
Washington	105,216			64,925	170,141
West Virginia	71				71
Wisconsin	133,001	206,387			339,388
Canada	57,680				57,680
Total:					
June 1940	17,422,860	3,857,962	2,155,414	4,046,338	27,481,874
June 1939	18,953,522	3,498,019	1,382,258	4,087,860	27,871,659

[1] Revised.

Grain

Weekly Weighted Price per Bushel of Reported Cash Sales, June 1940, With Comparisons of Monthly Averages

Wheat

Market and grade		Weekly averages				Monthly averages			
		June 3–8	June 10–15	June 17–22	June 24–29	1939 June	1940 April	May	June
		Cents	Cents	Cents	Cents	Cents	Cents	Cents	Cents
CHICAGO									
Hd. Winter	No. 2	82.0			82.0		75.1	110.9	104.8	82.0
	No. 3						78.2	109.1	91.2	
Red Winter	No. 2						74.7	113.4		
	No. 3				82.2		73.5	111.3	99.0	82.2
MINNEAPOLIS									
Dk. No. Spring Heavy	No. 1	86.1	84.2	82.9	82.5	84.0	109.4	102.0	83.6
Dk. No. Spring	No. 1	84.5	83.8	81.3	81.0	84.4	108.2	100.7	82.3
	No. 2	83.5	82.7	80.2	80.0	83.3	107.3	99.5	81.6
No. Spring	No. 1					82.0	107.1	98.7	
	No. 2						103.0	85.1	
Hd. Amber Durum	No. 2	74.1	74.5	72.0	74.0	76.4	99.1	88.6	73.9
KANSAS CITY									
Dk. Hd. Winter	No. 2	81.6	79.4	77.1	75.8	76.9	108.8	98.5	78.0
	No. 3	80.9	79.8	76.5	75.1	77.5	108.2	101.1	77.1
Hd. Winter	No. 2	80.1	79.5	76.4	74.6	70.9	105.7	94.7	76.3
	No. 3	78.3	78.5	75.6	74.2	70.8	105.1	96.3	75.7
ST. LOUIS									
Hd. Winter	No. 2		88.5			78.2			83.5
Red Winter	No. 2	88.4	88.5		82.0	73.4	111.2	104.3	87.4
	No. 3	89.0	85.7	82.7	75.5	72.0	108.8	107.7	84.0
SIX MARKETS [1]									
By classes (all grades)									
Hd. Red Spring		83.1	82.4	80.2	79.9	82.9	107.4	99.7	81.4
Durum		73.8	73.6	81.7	72.4	79.0	98.1	87.8	73.0
Red Durum		67.4	68.0	66.9	68.0	69.5	92.7	82.2	67.9
Hd. Red Winter		80.6	78.5	76.9	74.8	72.5	106.6	98.8	76.4
Soft Red Winter		81.9	82.6	77.0	72.9	67.7	106.2	101.2	75.2
All classes and grades		80.7	79.6	77.8	76.3	74.5	105.6	96.8	78.3
WINNIPEG									
(Cash close)									
No. Spring	No. 3	61.3	60.3	58.2	57.7	53.6	77.1	67.5	59.4

Corn

		June 3–8	June 10–15	June 17–22	June 24–29	1939 June	April	May	June
CHICAGO									
White	No. 2					57.4	70.1	75.8	
	No. 3		76.5				74.2		76.5
Yellow	No. 2	66.0	65.9	65.2	65.9	51.3	68.3	68.5	65.7
	No. 3	65.8	65.9			51.2	62.5	68.6	65.8
KANSAS CITY									
White	No. 2					56.1	64.5	72.5	
	No. 3						63.3		
Yellow	No. 2	68.2		65.5		50.3	65.5	68.9	66.6
	No. 3		67.5				62.1	67.5	67.5
ST. LOUIS									
White	No. 2		75.5		75.5	57.4	68.7		75.5
	No. 3								
Yellow	No. 2			65.5	51.6	62.8	68.1	65.5
	No. 3					59.2	71.2	
FIVE MARKETS [1]									
All classes and grades		66.3	65.6	65.1	65.0	51.3	63.7	67.6	65.5

Oats, White

		June 3–8	June 10–15	June 17–22	June 24–29	1939 June	April	May	June
CHICAGO	No. 3	35.4	35.2	35.3	34.3	34.0	43.1	40.6	35.1
MINNEAPOLIS	No. 3	32.2	33.3	33.6	32.2	31.2	39.7	36.6	32.6
KANSAS CITY	No. 3	36.5	34.0			30.8		38.5	34.8
ST. LOUIS	No. 3			35.8	33.5	43.6	40.7	35.3

Rye

		June 3–8	June 10–15	June 17–22	June 24–29	1939 June	April	May	June
CHICAGO	No. 2						50.0	73.5	
MINNEAPOLIS	No. 2	46.6	45.7	43.7	43.7	50.0	69.5	58.8	44.9

Barley

		June 3–8	June 10–15	June 17–22	June 24–29	1939 June	April	May	June
MINNEAPOLIS									
Malting	No. 2	52.8	51.1	49.8	50.1	59.9	57.8	57.4	51.2
Barley	No. 2	49.6	47.6	47.3	47.0	53.0	56.9	55.4	48.4
	No. 3	47.7	46.0	44.5	44.1	48.8	55.7	54.7	46.3

Flaxseed

		June 3–8	June 10–15	June 17–22	June 24–29	1939 June	April	May	June
MINNEAPOLIS	No. 1	185.7	175.1	167.5	168.2	181.1	210.8	196.9	178.4

[1] Duluth and Omaha included in wheat; Minneapolis and Omaha in corn.

Compiled from Chicago Daily Trade Bulletin, Minneapolis Daily Market Record, Kansas City Grain Market Review, St. Louis Daily Market Record, The Daily Omaha Price Current, and Duluth Daily Commercial Record.

Weekly Closing Prices of Futures, June 1940, With Comparisons of Monthly Averages

JULY FUTURES

Wheat

Market	Weekly averages				Monthly averages			
	June 3–8	June 10–15	June 17–22	June 24–29	1939 June	1940 April	May	June
	Cents	Cents	Cents	Cents	Cents	Cents	Cents	Cents
Chicago	80.6	80.7	78.3	77.2	72.9	106.9	93.4	79.3
Minneapolis	79.3	79.4	76.1	74.9	76.8	103.4	91.9	77.7
Kansas City	76.2	76.4	78.3	71.0	68.5	102.1	89.0	74.4
Winnipeg [1]	67.9	66.7	65.0	64.9	60.7	83.1	73.9	66.2
Liverpool					55.5			

Corn

Chicago	62.9	62.2	61.9	60.9	49.4	82.2	64.0	61.9
Kansas City	65.7	65.2	63.9	62.6	48.7	61.1	64.6	64.4

Oats

Chicago	33.2	32.9	31.6	30.9	33.0	37.5	35.4	32.2
Winnipeg [1]	28.7	28.7	27.4	26.9	29.6	34.4	30.8	28.0

SEPTEMBER FUTURES [3]

Wheat

Chicago	81.1	81.3	78.6	77.6	73.5	106.9	93.6	79.8
Minneapolis	79.9	79.8	76.5	75.5	77.2	103.4	91.9	78.0
Kansas City	76.4	76.8	73.6	71.8	69.0	102.0	89.1	74.8
Winnipeg [1]	70.2	69.2	67.4	66.9	61.8	84.7	76.0	68.5
Liverpool					60.4			

Corn

Chicago	61.6	61.0	60.0	59.0	51.0	63.2	63.9	60.4
Kansas City	60.8	60.2	57.6	55.0	49.7	61.6	63.4	58.7

Oats

Chicago	31.3	31.3	29.6	28.9	31.5	34.4	33.1	30.3
Winnipeg [1]	26.9	26.9	25.3	24.6	29.0	32.7	29.7	26.0

[1] Prices in 1940 converted at official rate which is 90.909.
[2] Conversions at current rate of exchange.
[3] October futures for Winnipeg and Liverpool.

Commercial Grain Stocks Report

[At the close of the week ended July 15, 1940 [1]]

United States Grain in Store and Afloat at Domestic Markets

Market groups	Wheat	Corn	Oats	Rye	Barley	Flax
	1,000 bu.	1,000 bu.	1,000 bu.	1,000 bu.	1,000 bu.	1,000 bu.
Atlantic coast	907	191	30	6	6	0
Gulf coast	1,471	149	220	1	0	0
Northwestern and upper lake	33,985	5,645	434	4,564	2,664	482
Lower lake	7,871	12,255	1,027	3,637	1,873	0
East central	3,956	966	189	224	125	0
West central, southwestern, and western	64,161	5,318	230	664	19	0
Pacific Coast	2,135	13	227	2	1,542	0
Total current week	114,576	24,537	2,369	9,098	6,229	482
Total previous week (revised)	95,507	26,064	2,947	9,382	6,143	704
Total year ago	114,024	26,401	5,339	7,847	6,762	287

United States Bonded Grain in Store and Afloat at Canadian Markets

	Wheat	Corn	Oats	Rye	Barley	Flax
Total current week	290	3,220	21	24	4	
Total previous week (revised)	326	2,668	42	24	9	
Total year ago	439	3,756	106	24	14	

Canadian Grain in Store and in Transit in Canada

	Wheat	Corn	Oats	Rye	Barley	Flax
Western country elevators and mills	65,214		3,047	687	2,831	281
Interior terminal elevators	14,654		26	0	0	0
Pacific coast terminals	16,985		95	11	40	0
Fort Williams and Port Arthur	71,818		636	580	1,297	186
Eastern elevators	60,283		1,166	304	793	62
In transit rail and lake	27,607		934	228	388	40
Total current week	256,651		5,905	1,811	4,315	569
Total previous week (revised)	255,824		6,055	1,816	5,704	575
Total year ago	92,051		9,415	2,454	5,950	137

Canadian Bonded Grain in Store and Afloat at United States Markets

	Wheat	Corn	Oats	Rye	Barley	Flax
Total current week	22,611		214	2,897	1,266	0
Total previous week (revised)	22,140		108	2,828	1,238	0
Total year ago	6,962		99	207	161	0

Total North American Commercial Grain Stocks

	Wheat	Corn	Oats	Rye	Barley	Flax
Current week	394,128	27,757	8,509	13,830	12,814	1,051
Previous week (revised)	374,797	28,732	9,152	13,950	13,088	1,279
Year ago	213,476	30,157	14,859	10,032	12,887	394

[1] Stocks as reported are at the close of business on the preceding Friday or Saturday.

Bonded stocks of other grain in United States markets, current week; from Australia, wheat 503,758 bushels; from Argentina, oats 6,992 bushels, rye 1,770,000 bushels.

Feed–Seed

Prices of Feedstuffs at Important Markets, June 1940 [1]
[Per ton, bagged, in carlots, sight-draft basis]

Commodity	Boston	New York	Philadelphia	Buffalo	Chicago	Milwaukee	Minneapolis	Cincinnati	St. Louis
Wheat millfeeds:	Dol.	Dol.	Dol.	Dol.	Dol.	Dol.	Dol.	Dol.	Dol.
Bran, spring	25.15	26.70	24.50	21.60	19.80	19.70	17.40		
Bran, hard winter									19.10
Middlings, standard spring	26.10	27.60	25.70	22.60	23.40	23.40	21.10		
Middlings, flour		30.00	29.45	25.75	26.25	26.25	24.00	20.40	
Shorts, brown									
Shorts, gray								29.05	26.20
Millrun									
Oilseed meals:									
Cottonseed meal (43 percent)					32.20	34.70			
Cottonseed meal (41 percent)	34.90	37.00		33.55	31.05	31.95	33.95	31.10	28.90
Cottonseed meal (36 percent)									
Linseed meal (37 percent)				28.50	29.70	29.25	26.25		31.40
Linseed meal (34 percent)	28.50	27.00						30.60	
Linseed meal (30–32 percent)									
Soybean meal (41 percent)	29.80		27.25	24.40	25.05	25.90			24.60
Miscellaneous:									
Gluten feed	24.70	24.85	23.40	22.45	18.35	19.50	21.55	21.70	18.60
Gluten meal				30.50	28.10	26.25	28.30		27.35
Hominy feed, white	28.60	28.55	27.25	26.50	23.90	23.50		23.60	
Dried grains, distillers	26.40			24.45	23.60			23.60	
Dried grains, brewers	23.25		22.45	20.75	18.00	18.00		21.50	18.60
Tankage, digester (60 percent)					41.25		41.25		
Meat scraps					41.25		41.25		41.25
Alfalfa meal, No. 1 (fine)					22.60		23.60		

Commodity	Kansas City	Atlanta	Memphis	Fort Worth	Denver	Ogden	Los Angeles	San Francisco	Portland, Oreg.
Wheat millfeeds:	Dol.	Dol.	Dol.	Dol.	Dol.	Dol.	Dol.	Dol.	Dol.
Bran, spring									
Bran, hard winter	18.60	26.55	20.70	20.20	20.25	22.10			
Middlings, standard spring									
Middlings, flour									
Shorts, brown	22.75								
Shorts, gray	23.60	32.90	27.75	28.00	26.75				
Millrun					21.75		24.90	23.80	20.00
Oilseed meals:									
Cottonseed meal (43 percent)				34.00	38.90	40.50		29.90	33.75
Cottonseed meal (41 percent)	30.10	32.60	24.90				24.00		
Cottonseed meal (36 percent)		29.75							
Linseed meal (37 percent)	30.90			35.45	35.80				
Linseed meal (34 percent)						44.25			
Linseed meal (30–32 percent)							20.30	24.00	31.40
Soybean meal (41 percent)	25.25			30.15		42.20	34.80	33.55	36.35
Miscellaneous:									
Gluten feed	18.35	26.60			23.65				
Gluten meal	25.10								
Hominy feed, white		25.25							
Dried grains, distillers									
Dried grains, brewers		25.45							
Tankage, digester (60 percent)	40.60								
Meat scraps	40.60								
Alfalfa meal, No. 1 (fine)	19.90						19.40	19.50	

[1] Prices are simple averages of 1 days' quotation each week.

Imports of Agricultural Seeds
Admitted Into the United States Under the Federal Seed Act

Kind of seed	June 1940	June 1939	July 1, 1939, to June 30, 1940	July 1, 1938, to June 30, 1939
	Pounds	Pounds	Pounds	Pounds
Alfalfa	600	2,000	[1] 3,376,400	3,263,600
Barley [2]			[2] 202,600	
Bean, Mung [4]	145,000		[3] 383,500	
Bentgrass [6]	9,300	1,800	[7] 155,000	196,000
Bluegrass, annual [4]			4,100	12,900
Bluegrass, Canada [4]			[6] 25,500	13,900
Bluegrass, rough [4]		44,000	[8] 857,300	710,000
Bluegrass, wood [4]			2,900	4,900
Brome, smooth	8,600		[5] 3,867,600	2,180,200
Buckwheat [4]	900		4,900	
Clover, alsike			[6] 440,500	7,100
Clover, berseem [4]				200
Clover, crimson	1,100	50,600	[6] 5,446,200	4,707,100
Clover, red	100		[6] 1,037,800	598,300
Clover, subterranean [6]		200	900	1,700
Clover, suckling [4]		1,400	34,700	55,300
Clover, white		12,100	[11] 781,900	2,384,900
Corn [5]	3,700		[6] 61,900	
Dogtail, crested [4]	2,200		[14] 14,500	2,000
Fescue, Chewings [5]	204,100	53,900	[4] 1,052,300	885,800
Fescue, meadow [4]			[15] 96,500	78,100
Fescue, other [6]	800	100	[4] 135,400	331,500
Flax [3]	55,000		[17] 55,500	
Foxtail, meadow [4]				200
Grass, Bahia [4]		900	[18] 44,100	21,600
Grass, carpet [4]			200	12,400

Imports of Agricultural Seeds—Continued
Admitted Into the United States Under the Federal Seed Act—Continued

Kind of seed	June 1940	June 1939	July 1, 1939, to June 30, 1940	July 1, 1938, to June 30, 1939
	Pounds	Pounds	Pounds	Pounds
Grass, Dallis [6]	3,800	1,100	[19] 106,400	144,300
Grass, Guinea [4]			[20] 60,000	28,200
Grass, molasses [4]			[21] 88,800	5,800
Grass, orchard [4]			[21] 287,800	1,726,700
Grass, rescue [4]		32,700	2,400	80,800
Grass, Rhodes [4]		1,000	[22] 91,800	91,800
Grass, velvet [4]			7,400	24,300
Kudzu [4]			[23] 9,300	7,500
Lupine [4]				17,400
Medick, black [4]			[15] 107,200	64,100
Millet, Japanese [4]			[24] 801,100	
Mixtures, alfalfa and alsike			[5] 15,900	
Mixtures, alsike and timothy			[5] 34,300	32,700
Mixtures, alsike, timothy, and red clover				7,400
Mixtures, clover		9,700		9,700
Mixtures, grass			[25] 75,400	300
Mixtures, sweetclover and wheatgrass [4]			[16] 1,500	
Oat [5]	204,900		[5] 10,801,600	
Pea, field [4]	300		[4] 700	
Proso [4]			[5] 6,000	
Rape, winter	120,000	507,900	[25] 5,401,100	7,348,300
Rye [5]			[5] 6,700	
Ryegrass, Italian			[20] 292,200	23,800
Ryegrass, perennial	5,600	35,200	[31] 661,290	622,100
Sourclover [4]			35,000	
Soybean [5]			[5] 2,900	
Sweetclover [6]		74,200	[32] 3,604,000	10,292,300
Timothy		100	[16] 15,300	1,600
Vetch, common			[5] 249,000	1,003,700
Vetch, hairy	66,600	826,900	[5] 2,751,500	6,498,700
Vetch, purple [4]			1,000	
Wheat [3]	3,300		[37] 287,700	
Wheatgrass, crested [4]	2,400	400	[5] 1,454,400	560,200
Wheatgrass, slender [4]			[39] 131,700	82,600
Total	833,300	1,658,400	44,470,800	44,095,000

[1] 2,777,900 pounds from Canada; 598,300 pounds from Argentina; 200 pounds from Australia.
[2] Not tabulated prior to Feb. 5, 1940.
[3] From Canada.
[4] Not tabulated prior to Feb. 5, 1940. Subject to Federal Seed Act effective Feb. 5, 1940. Countries of origin shown for importations entered after Feb. 5, 1940.
[5] 375,300 pounds from Hong Kong (360,500 pounds of Chinese origin; 5,000 pounds of Japanese origin); 6,300 pounds from China; 2,000 pounds from Japan.
[6] Subject to Federal Seed Act effective Feb. 5, 1940. Countries of origin shown for importations entered after Feb. 5, 1940.
[7] 126,800 pounds from Denmark.
[8] 2,945,600 pounds from France (115,400 pounds of Hungarian origin); 2,159,200 pounds from Hungary; 230,800 pounds from Germany (of Hungarian origin); 55,000 pounds from Poland; 55,500 pounds from Great Britain (32,700 pounds of Hungarian origin; 900 pounds of French origin).
[9] 98,300 pounds from France; 33,000 pounds from Rumania; 5,800 pounds from Canada; 100 pounds from New Zealand.
[11] 384,300 pounds from Hungary; 297,100 pounds from Poland; 43,200 pounds from New Zealand; 17,700 pounds from Great Britain; 7,500 pounds from Japan; 1,500 pounds from Canada (American goods returned); 600 pounds from Australia.
[12] 58,100 pounds from New Zealand; 3,800 pounds from Argentina.
[13] 2,200 pounds from New Zealand; 600 pounds from Great Britain (of Northern Irish origin).
[14] 303,500 pounds from New Zealand.
[15] From Denmark.
[16] 30,200 pounds from Hungary; 3,300 pounds from Canada; 1,300 pounds from Denmark; 300 pounds from Great Britain.
[17] 55,000 pounds from Argentina; 600 pounds from Canada.
[18] 200 pounds from Cuba.
[19] 20,700 pounds from Australia; 300 pounds from South Africa.
[20] 2,200 pounds from Brazil.
[21] 263,300 pounds from Denmark; 22,400 pounds from Japan; 900 pounds from Great Britain; 500 pounds from New Zealand (300 pounds of Australian origin); 100 pounds from Australia (of New Zealand origin); 100 pounds from Germany.
[22] 1,100 pounds from Australia.
[23] 4,300 pounds from Japan.
[24] 167,400 pounds from Australia.
[25] 67,600 pounds from Canada; 7,800 pounds from Great Britain.
[26] 1,500 pounds from Canada.
[27] From Hong Kong (Of Chinese origin).
[28] From Hungary.
[29] 4,067,700 pounds from Japan; 396,400 pounds from Great Britain (of Rumanian origin); 288,700 pounds from Switzerland (of Rumanian origin); 228,000 pounds from Rumania; 208,800 pounds from Hungary; 204,500 pounds from the Netherlands (165,500 pounds of Hungarian origin).
[30] 281,200 pounds from Argentina; 5,300 pounds from New Zealand; 4,200 pounds from Australia (100 pounds of New Zealand origin); 1,500 pounds from Northern Ireland.
[31] 322,600 pounds from Great Britain (238,700 pounds of Northern Irish origin; 77,900 pounds of Northern Irish and Danish origin); 297,600 pounds from Northern Ireland; 36,600 pounds from Denmark; 2,200 pounds from Australia (100 pounds of New Zealand origin); 2,200 pounds from New Zealand.
[32] 2,600 pounds from Canada; 300 pounds from Japan.
[34] 313,100 pounds from Canada.
[35] 16,000 pounds from Canada; 200 pounds from Great Britain.
[36] 160,900 pounds from Rumania; 88,000 pounds from Latvia; 160 pounds from Great Britain.
[37] 2,508,200 pounds from Hungary; 103,000 pounds from Latvia; 66,800 pounds from Sweden; 65,900 pounds from Czechoslovakia; 7,600 pounds from Canada.
[38] 284,400 pounds from Canada; 3,300 pounds from Brazil.
[39] 520,800 pounds from Canada.
[40] 100,900 pounds from Canada.

Cotton

Average Price of Middling 7/8–Inch Spot Cotton at 10 Markets, June 1931–40

Market	1931	1932	1933	1934	1935	1936	1937	1938	1939	1940
	Cents	*Cents*	*Cents*	*Cents*	*Cents*	*Cents*	*Cents*	*Cents*	*Cents*	*Cents*
Norfolk	8.80	5.24	9.50	12.23	11.99	12.14	12.80	8.57	9.67	10.34
Augusta	8.56	5.05	9.50	12.27	12.39	12.38	12.99	8.72	9.96	10.97
Savannah	8.61	5.12	9.40	12.15	12.06	12.18	12.82	8.48	9.80	10.57
Montgomery	8.16	4.87	9.08	11.82	12.17	11.87	12.48	8.41	9.47	10.31
New Orleans	8.86	5.18	9.33	12.13	11.96	12.12	12.50	8.47	9.45	10.54
Memphis	8.16	4.76	9.30	11.89	11.99	11.91	12.27	8.41	9.46	10.19
Little Rock	8.02	4.63	9.21	11.87	11.89	11.82	12.13	8.30	9.34	9.98
Dallas	7.91	4.80	8.97	11.72	11.60	11.51	12.16	7.96	9.09	9.80
Houston	8.54	5.11	9.27	12.15	11.84	11.86	12.47	8.30	9.37	10.09
Galveston	8.64	5.16	9.22	12.14	11.82	11.86	12.43	8.24	9.41	10.10
Average	8.43	4.99	9.28	12.04	11.97	11.97	12.50	8.39	9.50	10.29

Average Premiums for Staple Lengths of the Grade No. 5 or Middling, 7/8–Inch, July 5, 1940, With Comparisons

	New Orleans			Memphis		
	July 5, 1940	July 7, 1939	July 8, 1938	July 5, 1940	July 7, 1939	July 8, 1938
	Cents	*Cents*	*Cents*	*Cents*	*Cents*	*Cents*
No. 5 short staple	10.55	9.55	9.22	10.30	9.55	9.20
Length in inches	*Points*	*Points*	*Points*	*Points*	*Points*	*Points*
1 1/16	60	90	120	75	75	85
1 1/8	140	165	215	185	175	230
1 3/16	[1] 340	[1] 290	[1] 315	385	285	430
1 1/4	[1] 440	[1] 440	[1] 445	510	470	565

[1] Nominal.

Comparative Cotton Prices for May and June

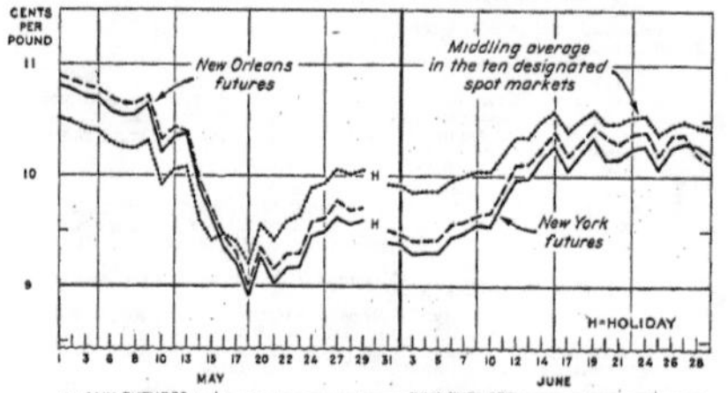

American Cotton Consumption

June 1940, With Comparisons

[Exclusive of linters]

Month	1913–14	1935–36	1936–37	1937–38	1938–39	1939–40	5-year average 1934–35 to 1938–39	Percent this year is of 5-year average
	Bales	*Bales*	*Bales*	*Bales*	*Bales*	*Bales*	*Bales*	*Percent*
Aug	432,350	408,325	575,014	603,617	559,409	628,448	513,061	122.5
Sept	442,435	450,647	629,767	601,305	533,399	624,902	501,963	124.5
Oct	511,923	552,840	651,086	524,188	543,857	686,936	559,001	122.9
Nov	456,356	512,312	625,794	482,976	596,416	718,721	539,516	133.2
Dec	456,262	499,773	694,841	432,326	565,627	652,695	521,983	125.0
Jan	517,299	590,484	678,786	433,258	598,132	730,143	570,243	128.0
Feb	455,231	515,977	665,677	426,866	562,580	662,659	530,288	125.0
Mar	493,354	550,641	776,942	512,626	649,940	626,331	594,504	105.4
Apr	499,646	576,762	718,975	413,169	543,187	623,893	544,099	114.7
May	466,744	530,894	669,665	426,149	606,090	636,467	540,642	117.7
June	446,145	555,449	680,521	443,043	578,436	556,529	528,286	105.3
Total, 11 mos	5,177,745	5,744,104	7,367,068	5,299,525	6,337,073	7,147,724	5,943,586	120.3
July	448,333	607,056	583,011	448,453	521,353	------	510,117	------
Total	5,626,078	6,351,160	7,950,079	5,747,978	6,858,426	------	6,453,703	------

Exports of American Cotton and Linters

Aug. 1, 1939, to July 5, 1940, With Comparisons

[Compiled from Government and commercial reports]

To—	Aug. 1, 1913–July 10, 1914	Aug. 1, 1936–July 9, 1937	Aug. 1, 1937–July 8, 1938	Aug. 1, 1938–July 7, 1939	Aug. 1, 1939–July 5, 1940	4-year average 1935–36 to 1938–39	Percent this year is of 4-year average
	Bales	*Bales*	*Bales*	*Bales*	*Bales*	*Bales*	*Percent*
Great Britain	3,447,430	1,182,942	1,600,199	469,003	1,987,093	1,167,554	170.2
France	1,086,063	715,620	756,570	895,928	835,698	644,414	129.7
Germany	2,843,554	748,150	881,826	457,567	33,456	737,740	4.5
Italy	480,688	408,906	533,381	304,942	611,279	410,558	148.9
Japan	339,484	1,574,986	656,130	876,157	913,170	1,160,979	78.7
Spain	280,119	------	278	14,500	293,677	55,586	528.3
Belgium	206,328	159,670	198,093	92,104	185,635	152,711	121.6
Canada	139,105	304,582	250,412	228,683	[1] 393,562	258,255	152.4
Other countries	340,272	582,372	926,290	647,309	1,087,822	696,902	156.1
Total	9,163,043	5,677,228	5,803,179	3,486,193	6,341,392	5,284,699	120.0

[1] To June 28.

Imports of Foreign Cotton

Aug. 1, 1939, to June 30, 1940, With Comparisons

[500-pound bales]

Country of production	1913–14	1935–36	1936–37	1937–38	1938–39	1939–40	5-year average 1934–35 to 1938–39	Percent this year is of 5-year average
Egypt	125,277	60,861	72,244	40,855	44,732	63,804	57,213	111.5
Peru	12,185	1,018	1,633	722	470	992	988	100.4
China	17,434	24,366	45,435	13,419	25,620	------	22,405	------
Mexico	74,476	3,387	27,391	29,186	20,014	12,184	17,023	71.6
India	6,984	44,046	77,208	43,263	40,429	70,910	45,408	156.2
Other countries	842	834	10,163	6,523	2,675	1,970	4,327	45.5
Total	237,198	134,512	234,074	133,968	133,940	149,860	147,364	101.7

American-Egyptian Cotton Consumed in the United States

Month	1930–31	1931–32	1932–33	1933–34	1934–35	1935–36	1936–37	1937–38	1938–39	1939–40
	Bales	*Bales*	*Bales*	*Bales*	*Bales*	*Bales*	*Bales*	*Bales*	*Bales*	*Bales*
August	754	1,130	1,600	1,128	882	1,957	1,366	769	710	2,128
September	690	1,802	1,811	898	349	1,727	1,682	728	610	2,128
October	944	1,322	1,671	1,085	952	2,001	1,750	731	651	2,110
November	1,041	1,042	2,104	940	740	1,764	2,107	594	931	2,296
December	1,177	1,315	1,694	1,119	742	1,825	2,029	599	1,353	1,833
January	1,472	1,041	1,184	1,143	929	2,242	1,797	377	1,734	2,208
February	1,641	1,068	1,178	1,210	808	1,922	1,820	235	2,037	1,608
March	1,745	1,145	1,207	1,288	817	1,729	2,081	389	2,398	1,278
April	1,722	713	1,125	1,154	1,097	1,669	1,684	357	2,160	1,226
May	1,381	612	1,142	963	1,417	1,413	1,497	409	2,222	1,164
June	1,413	457	1,607	996	1,351	1,372	1,304	492	2,209	1,359
July	1,379	788	1,485	611	1,259	1,755	980	507	1,623	------
Total	15,359	12,430	17,808	12,535	11,343	21,376	20,097	6,187	18,638	------

Linters consumed during the month of June 1940 amounted to 79,254 bales compared with 92,052 bales in May and 73,699 bales in June 1939. Linters consumed during the 10 months ended June 30 amounted to 976,255 bales in 1940 and 777,058 bales in 1939.

With the good yields now in prospect, total crop production is expected to be fully up to the average of the predrought years, and only slightly below production last year. But total crop production will not be as much above average as yields per acre because of the small acreage of crops being grown. After making an allowance for late plantings, for average abandonment of cotton, and for loss of other crops, the acreage to be harvested is expected to be only about 2 percent above the small acreage of last year and 3 percent below the average of the last 10 years—a period that includes the great droughts of 1934 and 1936. The acreage planted for harvest appears to be the fourth smallest since 1915. Potential crop production is also lessened by the reduction in the acreage planted to cotton and corn and the substitution of hay and legume crops of lower value per acre.

U. S. GOVERNMENT PRINTING OFFICE: 1940

9 780265 907290